THE WRITER'S WORKBOOK

Second Edition

The Writer's Workbook

Second Edition

Edited by

Jenny Newman, Edmund Cusick and Aileen La Tourette

Liverpool John Moores University

BLOOMSBURY ACADEMIC

First published by Hodder Education in 2000

Second edition published in 2004

This reprint published in 2010 by:

Bloomsbury Academic

An imprint of Bloomsbury Publishing Plc
36 Soho Square, London W1D 3QY, UK
and
175 Fifth Avenue, New York, NY 10010, USA

CIP records for this book are available from the British Library
and the Library of Congress

ISBN 978-0-3408-0965-5

This book is produced using paper that is made from wood grown in managed, sustainable
forests. It is natural, renewable and recyclable. The logging and manufacturing processes
conform to the environmental regulations of the country of origin.

Printed and bound in Great Britain by Good News Digital Books

www.bloomsburyacademic.com

CONTENTS

Part Three: Branching out

ABOUT THE EDITORS

Edmund Cusick has collaborated with Ann Gray to publish a volume of poetry, *Gronw's Stone* (Headland Publications, 1997). In 1998 he won the Housman Poetry Prize and was a runner-up for the Bridport Poetry Prize. He has also edited an anthology of contemporary women's poetry, *Blodeuwedd* (Headland Publications, 2002). He is Head of the Writing Department at Liverpool John Moores University.

As writer-in-residence at HMP Ford, **Aileen La Tourette** has taught creative writing and drama across the prison community. She has also taught creative writing at *The Big Issue* in London, on the Antioch University MA programme, and for the Arvon Foundation. She has published numerous poems and short stories, two novels, *Nuns and Mothers* (Virago, 1984) and *Cry Wolf* (Virago, 1986), a poetry collection, *Downward Mobility* (Headland Publications, 2004), and has had many plays on radio. She is a lecturer at Liverpool John Moores University.

Jenny Newman is the editor of *The Faber Book of Seductions* (1988), and co-editor of *Women Talk Sex: Autobiographical Writing about Sex, Sexuality and Sexual Identity* (Scarlet Press, 1992) and *Contemporary British and Irish Fiction: An Introduction through Interviews* (Arnold, 2004). Her short stories have appeared in *This Is, Pool* and *The London Magazine*. She has also written two novels, *Going In* (Penguin, 1995) and *Life Class* (Chatto & Windus, 1999), and many articles on contemporary British and North American fiction. She is a Reader in Creative Writing at Liverpool John Moores University.

ABOUT THE
CONTRIBUTORS

Dymphna Callery has been teaching drama and writing in higher education for 20 years. Her poetry collection, *What She Said and What She Did*, was published by Headland in 1997, and her book on physical theatre, *Through the Body*, was published by Nick Hern in 2001. She has had several plays performed in theatre and on radio. She is currently Head of Drama at the University of Wolverhampton.

Gladys Mary Coles has published nine volumes of poetry, including *The Echoing Green* (Flambard, 2002), *The Glass Island* (Duckworth, 1992) and *Leafburners* (Duckworth, 1986). Her major prizes include the Aberystwyth Open, the National Poetry Competition, the Scottish and Cardiff Internationals and a Welsh Arts Council writer's award. Her work has been anthologised by Faber, Cassell, Virago, Forward Prizes, and in *Twentieth Century Anglo-Welsh Poetry* (Seren Books, 1997).

Rose Flint is a writer and artist. She teaches creative writing at all age levels and works as an art therapist, using creative writing in healthcare. Her prize-winning poetry can be found in many magazines and anthologies, and she has had three collections of poetry published: *Blue Horse of Morning* (Seren Books, 1991); *Firesigns* (Poetry Salzburg, 2004); and *Nekyia* (Stride, 2003). She is lead writer for the Kingfisher Project in Salisbury Hospital.

James Friel is the author of *Left of North* (Macmillan, 1989), which won a Betty Trask award; *Taking the Veil* (Macmillan, 1990); and *Careless Talk* (Macmillan, 1994), which was nominated for the *Mail on Sunday* John Llewellyn Rhys Prize and a Welsh Arts Council bursary. He also writes for screen and radio. His adaptations of *Saigon, Villette, Cousin Bette, A Fairly Honourable Defeat* and *The Remains of the Day* have recently been broadcast on BBC Radios 3 and 4.

Dave Jackson is a freelance screenwriter and singer/songwriter. He has a BA in Imaginative Writing and an MA in Screenwriting, and won a

Lynda La Plante bursary in 1996. He has also sung with and written songs for post-punk indie bands The Room, Bennie Profane and Dust. With these bands he has released six LPs and a number of EPs and singles. Between 1980 and 1990 he recorded six John Peel sessions and toured in Europe, the USA and Canada. He still writes and performs with Dead Cowboys, who have recorded a mini-album of 'twisted roots' music.

PREFACE

There are many ways to become a successful writer, but there is no instant route to success. It takes talent, perseverance and luck. Today's writers may benefit from imaginative publishing houses, technology, global links such as the world wide web, hypertextual writing, new opportunities in the digital media, and other recent initiatives in the arts world. But funding for the arts is shrinking, the Net Book Agreement has been abolished, many independent bookshops have closed, and publishing, film and television companies are increasingly market-driven. Without advice and support, new writers can find themselves at a loss.

In both Britain and the United States, universities are playing a major role in the development of new writing. At Liverpool John Moores Centre for Writing we offer courses at MA and Ph.D level, and a three-year programme leading to a BA in Imaginative Writing. *The Writer's Workbook* is based on the latter, and this second edition has been revised and expanded in the light of student comments.

This is a book for people determined to write, and we strongly recommend that you work through the chapters in order. Only if you engage with its ideas and test its tenets through regular writing will you give yourself the chance to develop and expand your talent. We hope you enjoy it.

ACKNOWLEDGEMENTS

We would like to thank colleagues past and present at Liverpool John Moores University and elsewhere, whose inspiration and support enabled us to evolve the methods described in this book. We would also like to thank the student writers at BA, MA and Ph.D levels who used the first edition, and whose insight and enthusiasm have helped us expand and refine it.

Part One:
Exploring

1 THE WRITER'S JOURNAL

Jenny Newman and
Edmund Cusick

INTRODUCTION

The American poet Allen Ginsberg copied into his journal four sentences written by Kafka on 25 February 1912: 'Hold fast to the diary from today on! Write regularly! Don't surrender! Even if no salvation should come, I want to be worthy of it every moment' (Hemley, 1994).

The terms 'journal' and 'diary' both have their roots in older words for day, and both suggest a link with habit. There are as many sorts of journals as there are writers. Not only do the diaries of, for example, Franz Kafka, Sylvia Plath, Katherine Mansfield, Virginia Woolf, Anaïs Nin and May Sarton let you into the secrets of creative problem solving, but they are gripping and original works in their own right.

Some writers prefer to subdivide their journals into sections, or even into different books, while others find stimulus where diverse items rub shoulders. At the start of a recent workshop a group of MA Writing students took out their writer's journals, which included:

- an A3 artist's sketchbook
- a pocket camera
- a floppy disk
- a padlocked cash box filled with cuttings and scraps of scribbled-on paper
- a box filled with 5" × 3" cards in alphabetical order according to subject
- a spiral notebook
- a pocket cassette recorder
- a shoebox filled with swatches of material, old menus and postcards
- a ring binder with dividers between different projects.

The kind of journal *you* keep is a question of choice. The only type you might want to avoid is a year diary with each page divided into seven. If you like writing in notebooks, why not choose one small enough to fit in your bag or pocket, for use when you are on the move and want to catch fleeting impressions, and a second, larger journal to keep at home? Take time when selecting your notebook to find one that feels right: of good enough quality to last, but not too beautiful to use. Whichever type you choose, it should give you room enough to write freely, and to hold, if you wish, cuttings, photographs, letters or any other sorts of memorabilia you find evocative.

What follows are some descriptions of different kinds of journals, with writing exercises for each (in the boxes) to get you started.

THE ARTIST'S SKETCHBOOK

Good writing draws on effective description – the basic literary draughts-manship that allows you to communicate your sense impressions. Many writers believe, with William Trevor, that 'the only way you can create a character is through observation' (Plimpton, 1999). Yet daily life can bombard you with people, chatter, and rapidly changing surroundings which may at first seem irrelevant to, or a distraction from, your writing. Numbed by habit and overloaded with information, it is easy to miss revealing details. But the busiest street can become a source of inspiration if you cultivate the art of rapid scrutiny – from hairstyle to shoes, through hand luggage, clothes, complexion, jewellery and expression – in a single glance. You could start by buying an all-day bus or train pass, and use it for travelling with your spy notebook. Even places you pass on the way to work can be brought alive by observation. The nineteenth-century writer and artist John Ruskin, for example, complained that people never stopped to look at the sky. He himself claimed to 'bottle' skies in words as carefully as his father bottled sherries. Here is a sample from his 1857 diary:

> *November 1st:* A vermilion morning, all waves of soft scarlet, sharp at the edge, and gradated to purple. Grey scud moving slowly beneath it from the south-west, heaps of grey cumuli – between the scud and cirrus – at horizon. It issued in an exquisite day ... All purple and blue in distance, and misty sunshine near on the trees, and green fields ... Note the exquisite effect of the golden leaves scattered on the blue sky, and the horse-chestnut, thin and small, dark against them in stars (De Botton, 2003).

You need not restrict yourself to your sense of sight. If you learn how to listen, you will never find yourself recycling dialogue from soap operas or characters from the Sunday papers. Many people carry tales of the strangest, the most frightening or most exciting thing they have ever experienced, and are happy to share them. Pausing to jot down what you have heard or seen can sharpen your style and train your creative powers; or use a pocket-sized cassette recorder to catch what you see and hear, and transcribe the sentences you wish to keep at the end of the day.

- Go to a bus or railway station, an airport or ferry terminal. Observe groups of people meeting or saying goodbye. Deduce or imagine who they are and what their lives contain. Ask yourself, if these people were characters in my story, what would happen next?
- Write a description of a journey you take regularly, without mentioning street names, or directions such as right or left. Imagine you were instructing someone to take the same route, navigating only by landmarks. You may think you know the route backwards, but will probably find that you have to walk it again, discovering new things.

The freshness of immediate observation carries over into completed pieces of writing. For instance, a fantasy novelist may set her sword-and-sorcery trilogy in worlds far removed from this one, yet her accounts of warriors and knights might be drawn from her notes on Samurai weapons seen in a museum, or on medieval castles explored on holiday, or on her detailed descriptions of horses at a race meeting or farm. Whether you write about tower blocks, Caribbean islands or medieval monks, this is a way of learning the art of making your scenes real to your readers.

This exercise, adapted from one devised by Gladys Mary Coles, focuses on the often-neglected sense of touch, but it can be tailored to apply to the other four senses.

- In the middle of a blank page, write down a list of half a dozen things you dislike touching (e.g. liver, slugs, dead birds).
- To the left of this list, write a column of adjectives which tell your reader something more about these things (e.g. their texture, feel, specific kind or type). To the right of the list, write a column of verbs which illuminate the objects and your dislike of touching them. These verbs should be exact and energetic.

- Now think of what each item on your list reminds you of, thus creating a simile or a metaphor. This is the all-important leap into imagery.
- Following the same procedure, make another list of the objects/things you most like to touch (e.g. velvet or cat's fur).
- Take one of your tactile images, and use it as the starting point of a poem or story. Incorporate two more of your new images somewhere in the piece of writing. These images could act as symbols, and become the hubs round which the piece is structured (Sellers, 1991).

Even without a specific project in mind, you can be a magpie collecting ideas and images where and when you can. The material you do not use will sharpen your skills of observation and lay the foundations of your future writing. But you do not need to jot down everything you see or hear: it is more helpful to focus on how you perceive it. The moment you record a perception you start to structure it and organise its details. Once you become aware of how you apprehend your surroundings, you can start choosing the kinds of perceptions you wish to cultivate. As Anaïs Nin wrote in Diary VI: 'Every moment you can choose what you wish to see, observe or record. It is your choice. So you create the total aspect according to your vision. We have a right to select our vision of the world' (Rayner, 1986).

And if note-taking seems like a chore, remember the words of Thoreau: 'The writer who postpones the recording of his thoughts uses an iron which has cooled to burn a hole with' (Hemley, 1994).

Make a journey or extended field trip, perhaps as part of a writing group, to a place which is likely to yield inspiration: China Town or the Welsh mountains, Stonehenge or the nearest docks, the City of London or the Painted Desert – somewhere radically different from where you live. Immersion in a creative purpose for a day, or a whole weekend, can be a boost to your writing and give you the chance to share inspiration with fellow writers. Through cameras and notebooks, practise seeing places through different eyes.

THE DREAM CATCHER

Although you need to cultivate your analytical side by studying a range of techniques in your chosen form, there are times when thinking too hard can inhibit your writing. 'Writer's block' can be the result of straining for effect, or from a dread of being judged by an inner or outer critic. This fear can make the pen or word-processor freeze mid-sentence, or keep you away from your desk, or even take away the desire to write. To stop yourself from becoming self-conscious or over-critical of your early drafts, you need a place where you can play unobserved and gain the insight into your feelings which is essential for a writer. Try following the advice from Dorothea Brande (1986), and get into the habit of rising half an hour early, and without talking or reading the newspaper, start writing whatever words come into your head. These morning pages which, according to Brande, should not be reread, are invaluable in fostering a tendency to cast the experiences of the day ahead into words, and to transform the raw material of life into fictional shape.

John Fowles maintained that in his diary 'the novelist discovers his true bent – that he can narrate real events and distort them to please himself, describe character, observe other beings, hypothesise, invent' (Plimpton, 1999). When using your journal to unlock your creative self it is best to write for at least part of the time without worrying about grammar, punctuation or spelling. Even when not blocked, you need space to take intellectual and creative risks, to doodle or daydream, to rediscover your voice and experiment with different points of view. This is not the moment for meticulous editing. Brenda Ueland (1991) urges writers to 'keep a slovenly, headlong, impulsive, honest diary'. By writing the first thoughts that enter your mind, you will not be held back by a desire to please others.

Write as fast as you can for ten minutes. You may record your impressions of the day, or stay with a particular subject, or just write what comes into your head. As Brenda Ueland (1991) puts it, 'You will go straight to the point – be awkward, quick and insolent'. Remember you are free to write the worst rubbish in the world. To quote Ueland again: 'Be careless, reckless! Be a lion, be a pirate!' Write nonsense words if you feel like it and do not stop if you get stuck; just write the same words over again until new words come.

An uninhibited journal can become a source of dreams, plots and visions; or of snippets and images you are currently unable to develop but sense might someday be useful. If you record these when feeling inspired you can reflect on them over time, and pick out examples of what Henry James referred to in his notebook as 'the germ of a story' (Matthiesen and Murdoch, 2000). Some of these 'germs' will wither and disappear, but others will find their way into finished works of art. Virginia Woolf once grasped at an idea for a piece of writing which she described in her journal as a 'fin passing far out' (Woolf, 1953). This was her first intimation of her highly experimental novel *The Waves*, so she could not know precisely what it meant. On completing the novel five years after that initial 'sighting', she wrote in her diary for that night: 'I mean that I have netted that fin in the waste of water which appeared to me over the marshes of my window at Rodmell.'

Like Woolf and many other authors, the American novelist Norman Mailer believes in the relationship between the writer and his or her unconscious. The best way, he says, of gaining access to that realm is to sit at your desk each day without fail, 'even if you don't feel like it, even if you were enough of a fool to go out and get dead drunk the night before and you've forgotten what you were going to write' (Plimpton, 1999). Some writers tap their unconscious minds by pondering myths and legends which deliver ancient symbols and story structures (for more information about this approach, see Chapter 3, 'Working with myth'). Other writers see dreams as the gateway to their creative selves.

Keep a notebook beside your bed for a month. Write in it on waking, even in the middle of the night, and even if you cannot remember any dreams. Your recall of your dreams will almost certainly improve. But remember that if, like Henry James, you 'take a piece of paper into your confidence' (Matthiesen and Murdoch, 2000), it may be best not to show it to your friends – or only under special circumstances.

Some of the greatest works of imagination, especially in the Gothic and fantasy genres, have allegedly been inspired by dreams: Horace Walpole's *The Castle of Otranto*, S. T. Coleridge's 'Kubla Khan', Mary Shelley's *Frankenstein*, R. L. Stevenson's *Dr Jekyll and Mr Hyde* and George MacDonald's *Lilith*. For these authors, dreams are naturally creative, communicating symbols which can feed into their art. After reading their wonderful tales you might decide to follow the playwright Ionesco, who says of the mornings when he sits down to work, 'I let characters and symbols emerge from me, as if I were dreaming. I always use what remains of my dreams of the night before. Dreams are reality at its most profound, and what you invent is truth because invention, by its nature, can't be a lie' (Plimpton, 1999).

THE READER'S LOG

As you will see in Chapter 2, being a writer means endless, impassioned, meticulous reading, and every true writer's journal becomes a reader's journal. By reading in a certain way you learn what you enjoy and admire, and how to love other writers. As Tess Gallagher puts it, the love of other writers is an important first step (Sumrall, 1992).

It is crucial to read a book not only once for pleasure, but several times for technique. Keep a record of what you read, with notes on style, structure, plot devices or characterisation. Copy out lines or paragraphs from your favourite authors, read writers on writing, and collect those remarks which seem to illuminate the business of being an author. After a while you will find you are assembling your own writing manual, to turn to when you need guidance or wish to 'raise your game' in terms of technical achievement.

You can also read the journals of other writers and artists. In a recent article in the *Guardian*, the novelist William Boyd cited among his top ten diary-keepers the painters Keith Vaughan and Paul Klee, then Evelyn Waugh, Gilbert White, Cyril Connolly, Edmund Wilson and Valery Larbaud. Do not shy away from the journals of historical figures. James Boswell's diary, for instance, does not only tell us about how we once were, but about what we might be.

Copy into your journal or on to your word processor a paragraph from the work of a writer you admire, and from whom you would like to learn. Taking a piece of your work in progress, cast it syllable for syllable in the form of that paragraph. The sense of your work will be different from that of your chosen author, but you will have temporarily donned their sentence lengths and the rhythm of their prose.

It is the writer's job to consider not only a word's current meanings, but also its origin and history. Words, like us, relate to their next-door neighbours, taking their colour from – or fighting with – the company they keep. Each syllable has its own lineage and can, like a family, witness a dramatic change in definition and status across the centuries. Why not decide on the central image or symbol of your work in progress, narrow it down to a single word, and find that word in the 20-volume *Oxford English Dictionary*, which is the most extensive in the world? (Modern English draws words from languages as diverse as Arabic, Sanskrit, Dutch, Japanese and Gaelic.)

Write a one-paragraph biography of your word, then consult some dictionaries of myth and legend – for example, African, Greek, Hindu or Breton. Does your word crop up? And does the narrative structure of your one-paragraph biography, or of your work in progress, echo any of the myths?

THE THRESHING FLOOR

When the Victorian novelist Anthony Trollope began a new book, he prepared a diary, divided it into weeks, and kept it for the period he had allowed himself for the completion of the work. In it he entered, day by day, the number of pages he had written, so that if at times he 'slipped into idleness for a day or two, the record of that idleness has been there, staring me in the face' (Shaughnessy, 1993).

Though few contemporary novelists are as disciplined and prolific as Trollope, it is useful to know how long you spend on your writing – and how long you sometimes postpone it. While we may yearn for peaceful days in a study, it is possible that, as Henry Miller suggests, most writing is done elsewhere (Plimpton, 1999). If our lives are not 'ideal', we must snatch at what time we have: at a bus stop, on a plane, or waiting for the plumber to call. University writing tutor Maggie Butt devised a diary-type questionnaire about writing habits for her busy student writers. It included questions about the length of time they spent writing each day (or night), where they needed to be and at what time. Those who filled it in for the required six weeks not only learnt to identify the environmental and emotional conditions which helped them make best use of 'pockets of time', they also improved their performance over the module, gaining higher marks than those who did not see the project through to the end (Butt, 2001).

> ◦ Keep a faithful record of what and when you write over a period of six weeks. It will help you to plan your day, your week and your year, and to reshape it wherever you can around the times and activities which help your writing most.
> ◦ Compile a list of writing goals in your journal and measure your progress towards them. Try to make them achievable rather than wildly ambitious plans for instant success. Once you have begun to take your writing seriously, you have the rest of your life to reach them, though that lifelong commitment needs to be reflected at the level of each month, week and – ideally – day.
> ◦ If you regularly enter writing competitions, use your journal to keep a record of what you have sent where, the closing date, and what date the results are to be announced, so that your work may be released to send to a magazine, or to other competitions.

As well as being a record of productivity, journals can become an account of the progress of each work, from the 'fin passing far out', through the technical challenges encountered and overcome, to the gratifying moment when you reach the final full stop of the final draft. As Woolf used part of her journal for the writing exercises which helped her to develop her revolutionary style and methods of characterisation, so you too can use your journal to refine your technique, build up characters and analyse your successive versions. Sometimes, when we have been absorbed in a long piece of work, we lose perspective and need to revitalise our imaginations. If your writing feels flat, try turning for inspiration to another medium. You could, for instance, collect pieces of stirring music, or assemble photographs of your favourite sculptures. Look out for performances by theatre companies and dance troupes, or visit an art gallery. Many pictures tell a story, or trigger ideas by serving as a symbol of a hidden self.

- If one of your characters refuses to come to life, write a dialogue in your journal between her and you, asking questions about her desires, ambitions, feelings towards the other characters, and the events of the plot.
- Learn to randomise. You can draw on your jottings at any time by taking a sentence you have overheard and putting it in the mouth of one of your characters; or by using a neatly turned anecdote to add zest to a plot; or you could put a person you knew in childhood in a place you visited yesterday. All writing is to some extent a mosaic, a celebration of our mongrel selves; and besides, if a work of art was presented to you on a plate, how could you develop as a writer?

The novelist Paul Magrs suggests circling 20 words in a chunk of your work in progress and including them in a précis of that piece. To succeed you will need to write about your characters, themes and plot, without tying yourself down to essential facts which, as this is just an exercise, can be changed at will. The results may surprise you. As Magrs says, this sort of lateral thinking is like 'taking a biopsy of your writing mind. You can read the piece back and think: so that's what I think it's all about' (Bell and Magrs, 2001).

CONCLUSION

Journals satisfy different urges and meet different needs at successive stages in our writing lives. The important thing is to experiment until you find the best method for you, then commit yourself to it. There is no right or wrong way, as long as it helps you get what Guy de Maupassant called 'black on white' (Plimpton, 1999), and as long as you do not censor yourself. The greatest writers' diaries are marked by their dedication to the craft of writing, and also by their emotional honesty. When you look at yours in the weeks or even years to come, you may find a record of that truth, observation or unique perception which time might otherwise have muffled, and which you may just find yourself using to fuel your future work.

2 READING AS A WRITER

James Friel

'I read in order to find out what I know: to illuminate the riddle.'
Ozick (1988)

Reading is the best source of inspiration, the best means to educate yourself and to witness the skill of others – and to witness their disasters. It is through reading that you learn to structure a tale, describe character, delineate action, judge what works and what, for you, does not.

How you write, observed the novelist, John Gardner (1984), is always an expression – a consequence – of what you have learned from reading.

When you write, you are involving yourself in an enormous conversation with everyone else who has done likewise: you learn from them, correct in your own work what you dislike in the work of others, pay tribute to work you admire, establish yourself in a tradition.

There is always something else to read, always some author to discover, another genre to explore. One need not even make a distinction between highbrow and lowbrow, good and bad, or divide poetry from prose, screenplay from stage play. Reading is writing's mongrel muse.

Most twentieth-century novelists, for example, have been deeply influenced by the cinema. Graham Greene's thoughtfully made suspense novels owe as much to thriller-writing skills he learned from John Buchan and Robert Louis Stevenson as from the structurally elaborate and psychologically more probing fictions of Henry James. Samuel Beckett's doleful plays are partly inspired by the great clowns of stage and screen, and Woody Allen's comedies arise from a love of the far gloomier films of Ingmar Bergman. More recently, a film like Curtis Hanson's *LA Confidential* (1998) pays homage to Roman Polanski's *Chinatown* (1976) which, in turn, borrows its look and sound from *films noirs* of the late 1940s such as Howard Hawks' version of *The Big Sleep* (1948). James Elroy's novel, *LA Confidential*, owes much to the work of Raymond Chandler, author of *The Big Sleep*, and Chandler comes out of a tradition of pulp writing in the 1920s and 1930s. Pulp fiction may be termed lowbrow, but Chandler's work is also heavily influenced by the work of Thomas Malory and the legends of King Arthur.

Films, poems, stories, plays, song lyrics – whatever you read, have read or will read filters into your own writing. Reading – like everything else but much more so – is grist to a writer's mill. How your reading informs your writing is a complex process and worth investigating.

Be a replicant

The novelist, children's writer and film-maker Philip Ridley once made a list of 100 texts – comics, films, novels, songs and poems – explaining, 'If you were to make a replicant of me [*à la Blade Runner*] these should be the first things filed in my memory.'

Start with the first text that comes into your mind. Make a brief note of the possible reasons why that text surfaces before all others and then go on to do the same for a second or a third text. If it helps, let them emerge in a chain of associations: books you read as a child; books you read now; books you loathed, books you read as a guilty pleasure, books you have never read but feel as if you had, a poem you memorised when you were nine, a film that ever since has invaded your dreams, a song that instantly summons the past. Keep going. Work at this for half an hour. Allow film to follow book to follow comic to follow poem. Do not discriminate. See what comes. This is a map of your reading life, its suburbs, its palaces, its canals, its backstreets and its motorways.

Consider what you have done. What are the common features in your list? What obsessions does it reveal? What themes and interests?

Now, think of the things you have written, are writing and most wish to write. Do they tally? How? If not, why not? Are you writing something you would not read? Is that wise? Are you writing exactly what you wish to read? What is that exactly?

The questions, once they start, are endless. Let them keep coming. They should occupy you all your writing life.

INFLUENCES

But what about originality? What about your essential vision? What about being – intake of breath – 'influenced'?

'Influenced' by the best minds, the best styles and the most effective artists our civilisation has known? To be influenced by Proust? Perverted from true originality by the siren call of George Eliot? To read your contemporaries and find out what they are doing and you are not? Oh, how terrible the damage will be.

That said, certain writers can get into your bones. Iris Murdoch said she could not write a novel and read Henry James. She caught his style like measles. And some writers – the great stylists – can be infectious in this way.

This is not an argument against reading; it is an argument for reading more.

Change the words but keep the syntax

Dorothea Brande (1934) suggests that you choose any opening paragraph of a writer you either particularly admire or a writer of whom you fear you are too fond and whose voice may perhaps be drowning yours out.

In this case, you could take Jane Austen's *Emma*: 'Emma Woodhouse, handsome, clever, and rich, with a comfortable home and a happy disposition, seemed to unite some of the best blessings of existence; and had lived nearly twenty-one years in the world with very little to distress or vex her.'

Now change the words but keep the syntax. Stick to the same number of syllables and – if you can hear them – the same rhythms and stresses in the prose: 'Janet Worswick, pretty, witty and wise, with an exuberant heart and healthy constitution, loved to wrestle some of the best wrestlers in Llangollen; and had fought nearly forty-two men with hardly any to exhaust or defeat her.'

Austen may win hands down, but in the struggle you will have learned how balanced that syntax is, how rhythmic and precise it is, how freighted with irony. Isn't this useful knowledge? And you have a short piece of original writing that might go somewhere – who knows?

Try something similar with a writer you admire or whose influence you wish to exorcise.

You will only be influenced in a negative way if you read without understanding. Many writers avoid reading while involved in writing but this is wise only if writing all-out or in short bursts. If your work takes years to complete, are you really going to stop reading throughout that period – when you most need to investigate what it has to offer?

Take a leaf out of Flannery O'Connor's book and read good prose before you start a day's writing. Annie Dillard warms up by reading pure sound unencumbered by sense – Conrad Aiken's poetry or 'any poetry anthology's index of first lines'. Reading immediately before you write is what Cynthia Ozick calls 'priming the pump'. If what you read stains your own work, what harm? Work through it. Isn't this one of the reasons you redraft?

Never fight shy of letting your writing come out of your reading. There has always been a relationship between the two. Virgil modelled *The Aeneid* on Homer's epic poems and Milton's *Paradise Lost* is an attempt to equal in English what had been done in Latin and in Greek. Henry Fielding's *Tom Jones* is a homage to, and a satire of, the classical epic, and James Joyce's *Ulysses* uses *The Odyssey* for its very bones.

Writing comes out of reading either directly – Susan Hill writing a sequel to *Rebecca*, Leon Garfield completing Dickens' *Edwin Drood* – or sideways, as in Jean Rhys's oblique recreation of *Jane Eyre* in *Wide Sargasso Sea* or Peter Carey's reappraisal of *Great Expectations* in *Jack Maggs* or Kathy Acker's cut-and-come-again version of the same novel. Donald Barthelme rewrites *Snow White*. J. M. Coetzee rewrites 'the true tale of *Robinson Crusoe*' in his novel, *Foe*. The borrowings may be more deceptive – Angela Carter's comic reworking of all Shakespeare's plays into the plot of *Wise Children*, and Richard Beard's novel *Damascus*, where the author uses only words from one specific issue of *The Times*.

Suggestions for writing

Relying on the spine of a classic tale or simply dreaming up a back story to an established text can provide help and inspiration. Take a story which you know well – one that fascinates you (from the list you made in the 'replicant' exercise, perhaps) – and write a plan or synopsis in which you

- change the point of view
- change the location
- change the period.

Reread a novel or story that you already know well with the specific intention of taking note of either:

- clothing
- colour
- the weather.

Underline any reference to one of these subjects and notice how seemingly inconsequential details, often added primarily to make a convincing background, can also carry plot points and be an implicit means of developing character. See how a writer can use weather, building up heat so that the storm with which the tale ends is a natural culmination of details that had appeared incidental, or how, in Henry James's *Washington Square,* a woman who wears gaudy red gowns lightens her wardrobe as the story goes on, until the last chapter when she is in bridal white – but we know that she will end her life a spinster. The details work at a subliminal level but that is where they work best.

Sharpen your eyes and ears as a reader. Nabokov (1980) would have you draw Anna Karenina's hair from Tolstoy's description, or the carriage ridden in by Emma and Leon in *Madame Bovary*.

- Find the screenplay of a film and either imagine or storyboard two or three scenes before watching it, deciding where you would place the camera, use music, instruct the actors. Compare your ideas with the finished product.
- Why not take the first page of an existing novel – or even a sample of your own prose – and adapt it for stage or screen? For prose writers this can be an effective editing exercise, cutting a scene down to its essentials. You can, of course, do the reverse: take a script and novelise it.
- Take down from your shelves six books – ones that you have yet to read – and, after studying the blurbs, reviews or anything else on their covers, write what you imagine might be the opening paragraphs, then compare your own attempts with the actual openings. This is an excellent way of kick-starting a piece of writing and investigating another writer's technique – and your own. It is particularly good when considering genre fiction such as crime or sci-fi. Your own version may be different – better, even. If so, you are free to continue with it.

- A not dissimilar exercise is inspired by Raymond Queneau's *Exercise in Style*, a collection of 99 short pieces that recount the same banal incident in different styles. The narrator bumps into a long-necked man on a bus and later sees him in a train station in the company of a friend who fixes a button on his coat. Before you read this fascinating, witty book, recount the above incident as a chapter in a romantic novel, a spy story, a detective story, a western, a Greek tragedy.
- Will this more self-conscious way of using your reading take the pleasure out of a favoured leisure pursuit? Initially, yes, but what is gained is knowledge, insight, confidence, ideas and inspiration. Reading for a writer is a form of work, another way of thinking about writing. A writer is always hunting, looking to snatch or steal, discovering what to avoid and what to make their own.

THE PRACTICE OF POETRY

In his last collection of poetry, *The Path to the Waterfall*, Raymond Carver began to write out passages from Chekhov's stories, turning the prose into poetry simply by using line-breaks. A. S. Byatt, in her novel

Possession, takes a passage from James's *The Golden Bowl* and, with a little tampering, turns it into poetry 'written' by her hero, a fictional Victorian poet. This exercise is useful not only to poets but to prose writers. Practising poetry can teach prose writers a great deal about the heft of individual words, about placing them in a sentence to gain effect, poise, spin. Simply write out the prose and insert a line-break where you would naturally pause if it were being spoken aloud.

In order to do the above exercise you will have to read your work aloud, or at least mumble it. Do not fight shy of doing this. It is also a way of making your words other: hearing them outside yourself. If you write for children but cannot keep their attention, how else are you going to learn what pleases them? Learning what captivates an audience is not so dissimilar to learning what captivates the individual reader. May Sarton (1985) considered the reading of a poem to an audience as similar to making a final draft.

People say that the internet is putting an end to reading. How can this be when the internet is almost nothing but text? It is a great store of knowledge, and think of all the things a writer needs to know. As Annie Proulx put it, 'I need to know which mushrooms smell like maraschino cherries and which like dead rats ... [and] that a magpie in flight briefly resembles a wooden spoon' (New York Times News Service, 1990).

You can apply the same system to surfing the net as you do to a bookshelf or encyclopaedia or dictionary. Graze. Surf – or what Proulx calls 'road drift'. The rules are simple: always take a branching side route, stop often, get out and listen, walk around, see what you see.

DO AS YOU WOULD BE DONE BY

The writer Nathaniel Benchley said he found bookshops too depressing to enter. All those books – each an attempt at immortality – resting on the shelves unread, unloved.

You must read them. You must love them. Who else will keep the art of reading alive if not writers? Rescue the past. Seek out your books and writers that are unloved by others. Adopt them. Rediscover the best of those we have left behind and out of print. One day you might be among them, waiting for a future reader, a future writer, to hunt you out.

CONCLUSION

Read the world as if it were a text. Consume it and find words to convey the experience of it, then weave those words into stories. This is what a writer does, isn't it? You are turning the world into text, so that there is ever more to read, ever more to write.

3 WORKING WITH MYTH

Edmund Cusick

INTRODUCTION

Myths are the first stories, the mother and father of all the stories that follow. The age of myths is measured not in years but in thousands of years. Within myths are experiences and intuitions so powerful that they grow while being told and retold down the generations. Myths are stories which encode intuitions of the way the world is. Every culture has myths to explain our first beginnings: the Yoruba myth of first men coming to earth on a ladder spun by a spider, or the Indian story of Yama and Yami, the first man and woman, or the Hebrew story of the Garden of Eden. ˇ

Why use myths? Why breathe oxygen? We have no choice. To tell stories is as natural to us as breathing. We are, in a sense, made of stories: every culture in every age has told them, and our stories form our understanding of ourselves and of the world. We may have swapped the campfire for the soap opera, tales of marvels for gossip and urban legends, but our hunger for stories remains as keen as ever. Even soap opera plots develop mythic dimensions: the body under the patio, the secret act of incest, can, for a week or a month, grip the collective imagination.

Compulsive stories

In your journal write, in note form, any story you have heard in the last fortnight. Try to think of one which, after you heard it, you felt you had to tell to someone else (it could be, for example, a film plot, a joke, a twist in a TV serial or an anecdote about someone you know). What is its appeal? Surprise, humour, shock? Jot down other stories you have told more than once, particularly any you may have retold over several years. What was their appeal?

As individuals we arrange the way we understand ourselves, our lives and those whose lives have touched ours into stories for our letters, conversations and diaries. At a deeper level still, we weave stories in our heads, sometimes without realising it: personal myths of where we have come from, of what one day we may achieve, of the fateful events that have led to our greatest triumphs or disasters. We live within these stories, shaping our sense of our lives, continually composing and recomposing. To be aware of this is one step towards fiction writing.

Before writers there were tellers. All literature has its roots in oral tradition. In storytelling there is a tradition known as 'the ladder to the stars'. The best illustration of this is a night given over to storytelling, during which there is a natural progression from personal anecdote to tales of the family and ancestors, from tales of the ancestors up to heroes, from those of heroes to the deeds of the gods and the great story of the creation of the world. Even for those who have no interest in oral storytelling, the personal can serve as a gateway into understanding and working with myth. The key is being able to find a point of imaginative contact where the universal can, for you, become personal.

Deceit

Tell a lie about yourself to someone else. About your history, your family, your life experience. Introduce yourself by a false name; invent an imaginary sister; hint at your time in the Foreign Legion. But let the name, the life story, the scandalous cousin, be something you wish were true, or that you feel *should* be true: something that is true on the inside, if not on the outside. Go on. Try it. You can always confess later. Then again, you might decide not to.

Life history

Write the story of your life in exactly 100 words. Each word must be only one syllable. It is tempting to cheat a bit, but follow these rules exactly. Read your story back to yourself. It is your life, stripped to essentials. It can be surprising how a deep narrative, an underlying pattern, comes through.

Find out as much as you can about your family history, for as many generations as you can trace. Do you have family legends about members living or dead? If so, what do they say about you as a family, and why do you think those stories have been passed down?

Roots

In your writer's notebook, try to summarise the most significant movements and events in your family history, and note any narratives within it – perhaps of a distant relative – which grip your imagination. How do you feel about this inheritance? Is it one you identify with or wish to pull away from? Can you think of a story that sums up your attitude to life – for example, a story of one thing you have done, that you would like your descendants to tell about you? If so, record it.

Memory

Write in note form any myth or legend you remember, if only roughly. Why does it stick in your mind? Try to remember where you first heard it, and any other sources where you have come across different versions. Note anything that intrigued you or left you puzzled or dissatisfied. If you told the myth to someone else, how would you expand on these points to make sense of them?

Myth and the self

Choose any myth or legend you remember, and write it as a story of three or four pages. Begin with the word 'I', and make the second word the name of its heroine or hero. Take the central character and become them, imaginatively, so that the whole story is told in the first person.

FINDING MYTHS

Books of myths and legends from a range of traditions are widely available: one fine example is Kevin Crossley Holland's *The Norse Myths*. Note that traditional stories are often designed to be told orally. When written they look skeletal – mere summaries of the action and some lines of dialogue – such as the *Mabinogion* and Graves's *The Greek Myths*. Do not be disappointed. The gaps are there to let you, the teller or writer, use your imagination. The skeleton contains all you need to bring the story to life in your own way.

Read myths from different cultures: Indian, Irish, Greek, Welsh, Egyptian. You will find that some seem more in tune with your imagination than others. If there is a place which figures in your story, or your family's, start there. If you have links with India, for example, you could begin with the *Ramayana*. Browse through your books until you find a character or incident which 'grabs' you. Some bodies of mythology have less to do with a nation than with a religion. The Bible, for example, is one of our most influential sources of mythology. Read it in the Authorised Version, beginning with the Book of Genesis, with its stories of the creation of the world, the encounters between the sons of God and the daughters of men, Cain and Abel, and Jacob wrestling with an angel.

Cinema and myth

See Chapter 7 on 'Writing for screen and television', and on the archetypal patterns often used in screenplays. There are countless examples of myths influencing films, but look, for example, at *Blade Runner, Devil's Advocate, The Warriors, The Blue Lagoon, Raiders of the Lost Ark, Splash* and *The Matrix*. The more myths you read, the more you will recognise mythic plots.

Heroes

Almost all bodies of myths have a hero, male or female, whose birth and childhood are surrounded by marvels. As they grow up their epic deeds (often involving a quest for some precious goal, which may take years to fulfil) generate further material for stories. From Jason and the Argonauts, Philip Pullman's Lyra, J. K. Rowling's Harry Potter and J. R. R. Tolkien's Frodo (Tolkien was himself a professor of heroic Anglo-Saxon literature) to Luke Skywalker and Lara Croft, the hero is one of the most magnetic figures in fiction. The fantasy genre, in both books and computer games, abounds in heroes, as do most other kinds of genre fiction, including love stories, thrillers and detective stories. To create a hero is one of the most liberating and enjoyable forms of imaginative invention.

Birth of a hero

Invent a hero, writing notes on his or her origins, gifts, mission, friends and principal opponents. Have fun. If you can both enjoy your hero and take her seriously, the chances are that your reader will do both also. Remember that not all heroes are entirely likeable – many have one or more vices, which complicate their nature, and the reader's reactions.

The following exercises are based on heroic narratives of Greek myths but can be adapted to suit your favourite material.

Entering the myth: heroes and victims

Read the story of the labyrinth and the Minotaur in Robert Graves's *The Greek Myths*, from its beginnings with Poseidon, Pasiphae and the bull. Imaginatively enter the plot as Ariadne or Theseus. Choose one moment and write his or her thoughts. Then choose another character at that same moment: King Minos, Daedalus, Pasiphae – the Minotaur itself – and write *their* thoughts.

Transforming the myth

Think of ways you could use the story with your own themes and characters. What would the labyrinth be in your dreamscape, the landscape of your imagination? An underground rail network, a maze in a country house, a tormented soul with a complex and bewildering psyche, an alien spaceship, a huge corporation where no one trusts anyone else? Who would you have explore such a place and what is the most shocking monster that might be trapped there? Use this as a starting point for a poem, screenplay or story. Though you do not have to follow the myth in every detail, returning to it will often inspire you.

Myth, legend and landscape

The land we live in is inhabited by stories. This is reflected in the many sites which bear Arthur's name or are in other ways associated with Arthurian legend, which has survived from Celtic times to the present day, passing from story to painting to poem to novel and film. Both the Arthurian paradise of Avalon and the Celtic underworld Annwn were believed to have a hidden location somewhere around the islands of Britain. Many other sites are associated with ancient legends: Carmarthen, Scone, Iona, the Giant's Causeway, Stonehenge, Glastonbury, Nottingham, Tintagel, Loch Ness and Pendle Hill. There will be legendary places near you – with haunted tower blocks, black dogs, buried treasure and places you must avoid at all costs at midnight. Find them out. It may help to read books such as Colin and Janet Bord's *Atlas of Magical Britain* and Uan Begg's *On the Trail of Merlin*. Use your holiday travels to collect more stories; it is another way of getting to know a place. This can prove rewarding whether you travel in Britain or abroad. Crete, for example, is the site of the labyrinth, Rome has its legends – and tourist souvenirs – of Romulus and Remus suckled by a she-wolf, and the dragon on the Welsh flag belongs to one of the oldest stories of Britain.

Local legend

Find a local site famous for a legend or folktale: for example, Weyland's Smithy in Oxfordshire. The story of Weyland can be read in Geoffrey Ashe's *Mythologies of the British Isles*. Read it at the site, or go in a group and let one person tell the legend to the others. Make the imaginative leap of seeing and hearing the characters from the story at the scene around you. If you do go in a group, try not to talk about your creative ideas until you return. Jealously guard your inspiration.

MYTH AND SYMBOL

Myth is more than a body of stories, it is a way of associating with an inner, intuitive order rather than the cold logic of fact. It is peculiarly responsive to both the creative imagination and the unconscious.

Myth, though often transcribed in prose, resembles those works of poetry which are driven not by the dictates of outer realism – the world as we see it – but rather by the compulsions and fears of the world *behind* our eyes. The narrative can seem at times no more than a setting for images – grotesque, arresting, beautiful – thrown up by our desires or dreams. Two obvious examples are images of magical transformation, and the strange combinations of human and animal which run through most mythic traditions. Such myths offer a gateway into the worlds of symbol (a shape borrowed from the outer world but charged with inner meaning) and magic (the ability to abandon the laws of causality for the reign of supernatural order). The story of Blodeuwedd, in the fourth branch of the *Mabinogion*, is a tale driven by magical symbolism: its heroine is transformed from flower to woman to owl, and her spouse, in the moment of death, becomes an eagle, and is then charmed into human form once more.

The exercises that follow are different from those elsewhere in the book: they are exercises in imagination, rather than in writing *per se*. They may seem strange, tiring or, to use an older word, *weird*. Try them anyway.

The shapechanger

Choose a time when you can relax completely. You may find that the moments of going to sleep or waking are best. Imagine yourself as an animal – any animal – a leopard, an eagle, a cat. Move through your five senses and feel them as you would in animal form. Discover the joys of swimming, flying, crawling, hunting.

Dreams

Gather material from your dream diary (see Chapter 1). Look out, in particular, for elements that do not stem directly from your daily life. See if the stories of your dreams exemplify your personal myths. You may find Carl Jung's *Man and his Symbols* useful.

The inner room

Systematically construct your perfect place. It might be a palace, beach, church or temple, a hillside or a wood. You can start from a place you know, but feel free to adapt it radically. You cannot do this at one go. Return to it, perhaps daily or nightly, enjoying the peace or exhilaration it offers. After a while it will develop its own energy, its own certainty, and you will not need to put effort into constructing it. Discover new things in it. Design a gate or doorway which you open and close behind you as you enter or leave it. Take time to create this doorway, so that it too reflects your character and tastes.

CONCLUSION

You will see how Chapters 6 and 14 refer to basic story patterns, and how Chapter 8 uses fairytale, another kind of traditional story. These models have not been chosen by chance. Myths are at the core of literature, and you cannot go far without rubbing shoulders with them, though you can do so without recognising them. Many great works of art draw on their resonances, sounding depths which narrowly realistic writing cannot do. Try looking at John Burnside's *Swimming in the Flood*, Seamus Heaney's translation of *Beowulf*, James Joyce's *Portrait of the Artist*, Ted Hughes's *Birthday Letters*. Read Charlotte Brontë, Vicki Feaver, Hilary Llewellyn-Williams, Rose Flint or Michèle Roberts.

If you strain to evoke symbolic echoes they will elude you, or seem forced. But if you open your imagination, starting, perhaps, with the exercises here, and seek out myth for its own sake, the depth of your knowledge will resonate with your readers, even without your being aware of it.

Part Two: Advancing

4 RHYTHM
Edmund Cusick

Listen:

It was the best of times, it was the worst of times.

What in heaven's name brought you to Casablanca?
My health. I came to Casablanca for the waters.
The waters? What waters? We're in the desert.
I was misinformed.

I have been one acquainted with the night.

The deaths of stars have made us.

You know how to whistle, don't you, Steve? You just put your lips together and blow.

To be or not to be, that is the question.

Have you read these lines on the page? Now read them aloud. Feel their weight, their movement. Try curving your palm very lightly over your larynx as you do so – just enough to feel the vibration of your voice.

This chapter is concerned with the substance of words, for your writing has body as well as soul. How do words reach your audience? They become most real, most sensuous and powerful, in the vibrations generated by your vocal chords which sound on the eardrum of your listener, in the movements of throat and tongue through which your reader's body follows your intent. From this movement comes meaning, feeling, pleasure. This is the foundation of both writing and music, chant and song. Fine writing – your writing – is the making of music out of words. It must be carried through the senses before it can delight the mind, and those senses embody this delight. Even when we read 'silently', an echo of the physical sound still plays in our mind, and a vestigial pattern of its shape moves across our throat.

Though this aural dimension is powerful, it works for the most part without the reader, or hearer, realising it. It is a subtle effect which is registered by its results only, while the devices through which it is created remain largely unconscious to the audience. The most important thing this chapter teaches is how to bring that unconscious dimension into conscious understanding and control.

The first stage of this process is to get used to reading aloud. None of the techniques, or exercises, this chapter contains may be accomplished by silent reading or silent writing. They make sense only when spoken aloud.

When we make language to remember, to sing and cherish, we use heightened language – language that is more enjoyable to the ear than normal speech, because it is more richly and interestingly wrought. One obvious example is the use of rhyme. Such techniques are most obvious in poetry, but are also used, for example, in advertising – think of a slogan which has stuck in your mind, and the chances are that it employs one or more of the devices we usually think of as belonging to poetry. Rhythm is such an art.

Learning control of rhythm is one of the most satisfying parts of the writer's journey. But it is also one of the most technical, involving hard work, particularly at first. Learning the basics is a practical art, like learning to play the guitar, or drive a car. Like these, it can seem impossible when you first set out – hours of practice with several things to remember all at once. There are, sadly, no shortcuts to competence. This chapter assumes that you are prepared to invest the hard work. The reward will be a fine one. You will enrich your understanding and appreciation of the literature you read. You will learn new ways to influence a reader. Most of all, you will make your work sound professional.

A word of caution: if this subject is new to you, you are extremely unlikely to take it all in at one reading! Take your time, rereading the chapter as often as you need to.

STAGE 1: UNDERSTANDING RHYTHM AND RECOGNISING STRESS

English is a stressed language. That is to say, in English, some syllables receive more force, or stress, than other syllables. They are pronounced more fully. In the word 'secondhand' for example, we clearly hear the first syllable, 'sec' but the next syllable, when the word is said naturally, shrinks to a brief, unimportant sound – more like '-nd' than 'ond'. What we hear sounds roughly like this: SECK'ndHAND. You do not pronounce the vowel in the second syllable; rather, it shrinks away. Try saying it another way, with more force on the second syllable than on the other two: s'CONDh'nd. That pronunciation sounds strange because it breaks the pattern of stress we are used to. Stress changes the sound of words: compare, for example, the names Lauren, Loren (as in Sophia Loren) and Lorraine.

In *Lauren* the first syllable is given emphasis but the second syllable is not, giving a sound we could roughly describe as 'LORRun'. In *Loren*, the second syllable is emphasised, so that it sounds a bit like L'rrEN. Similarly, in *Lorraine* the second syllable carries the emphasis, leading to a sound like LrrAYNE.

Linguists refer to the emphasised syllables (in block capitals above) as *stressed*, and the other lighter, smaller ones as *unstressed*. In poetry, rhythm is created by the arrangement of stressed and unstressed syllables at regular intervals in a line, so that 'heavy' and 'light' sounds develop a regular pattern when spoken aloud, similar to the way that music establishes a beat – 'ONE two three four'. Understanding – being able to hear – the difference between stressed and unstressed syllables is the keystone of all rhythm. Without this skill you can go no further, so practise listening, and recognising the pattern of stress in individual words, before you go on to the next stage.

Metre

The name given to a regular pattern of stressed and unstressed syllables is metre. Whereas we use the word 'rhythm' to describe the general sense of a 'beat', metre is a more precise term which implies that the beat can be notated exactly. While all literary forms can use metre, the terms used to describe it are drawn from the study of poetry. Learning how to follow such exact notation – to write a line of verse syllable by syllable, according to a set pattern of rhythm (that is, of patterns of stressed and unstressed syllables) – is the next stage of your training in controlling sound. Note that this chapter is not intended as an introduction to metre as it is studied by critics and scholars. I will make some reference to metrical terms, but the aim of this chapter is practical rather than critical: to help you to become aware of how rhythm works in your own writing.

STAGE 2: RECOGNISING RHYTHM: PATTERNS OF STRESS

As in music, so in poetry – most artists do not attempt to invent a rhythm entirely from scratch, but use one which has proved its value, and will already be familiar to an informed audience. One useful example of rhythm is found in the limerick. When we hear the line, 'A clumsy young plumber named Jock', we know what to expect – even if we think we know nothing about poetry, rhythm or metre. We are unconsciously responding to the rhythmic cues we have learned from hearing other limericks.

'There was a young girl from Biarritz' and 'A short-sighted farmer from Wick' sound right. They fit a 'tune' we already have in our heads, and we gain pleasure from the fulfilment of our expectations. 'There was a traffic warden from New York' and 'There was a lady from Johannesburg' do not sound right. Because the limerick has an established metrical form we expect to hear stressed syllables in certain places. All rhythm is based on this principle, and is a continual intercourse between what the reader unconsciously expects and the sound patterns which you actually provide.

In learning to write in rhythm, the first stage is to learn to follow such a model. Even if you always want to be original, the only way *at first* to acquire the art of rhythm is to learn to follow such patterns – just as the most adventurous driver had once to learn how to go up and down through the gears, and every pianist had to learn their scales.

There are, sadly, no rules in English as to which syllable will be stressed. It is generally true that abstract monosyllables – prepositions and articles such as 'a', 'the', 'an', 'of', 'with' – do not bear stress, whereas 'concrete' monosyllables, for example, *rope, bark, knife* and *white,* are stressed. But for words of more than one syllable, each one is different, and you must train your ear to hear where the stress falls. This takes time and hard work, but will pay off many times over. The readers you most need to please – editors, publishers – will, to a woman, have acquired this training till it works as smoothly as an instinct. This is particularly true in poetry, where reading a few lines of your verse will be enough to reveal whether or not you can control rhythm.

Iambs

The mostly commonly used metre in English verse is called *iambic*. Iambic metre consists of one unstressed syllable followed by a stressed one, and so on through the line. Some English words are natural iambs, as below (stressed syllables are in bold):

depart today about deflect connive recall

Some longer words form two iambs: that is, two units (which are also known as feet), each of an unstressed syllable followed by a stressed syllable:

Ridiculous admonishment, reiterate

as do some phrases:

to hear the sound,   go through the gate

It is possible for whole sentences to accidentally fall into iambic metre. Say these aloud and you will hear the rhythm in them: I **had** to **go** in**side** to **get** a **coat**. He **comes** there **every morn**ing **after twelve**. The **girl** be**gan** to **comb** her **wavy hair**.

Trochees

Another metre, the trochaic metre, has a similar balance of stress and unstress, but falling in the opposite order – a stressed syllable followed by an unstressed one.

Bargain **liv**er **short**age **or**ange **eag**le

are all natural trochees. English sentences can naturally – accidentally – be in trochaic metre without sounding too unusual.

Underneath the **stairs** it's **get**ting **cold**er.

Flights are **all** de**layed** to**mor**row.

Sam is **com**ing **down** from **Tex**as.

Iambic pentameter

A line of poetry which consists of five iambs is called *iambic pentameter*. As each iamb has two syllables, there is a total of ten syllables in a line of iambic pentameter, and these syllables are alternately unaccented (unstressed) and accented (stressed). This metre has dominated English poetry since the Renaissance, and poets from Shakespeare to Jackie Kay, Elizabeth Barrett Browning to Philip Larkin, have employed it. Both the sonnet and the ballad are based on the use of iambic pentameter, and we can hear it, for example, in Christina Rossetti's sonnet:

Re**mem**ber **me** when **I** have **gone** away

Gone **far** a**way** in**to** the **silent land**

Practise speaking this rhythm and you will feel its power to shape a thought: to offer it a balanced and measured progression which is more pleasant to listen to than the random, uneven scattering of stressed syllables in everyday language. At the same time, iambic metre has proved so enduring because it is the rhythm which most closely echoes English speech; that is, it represents only a limited reordering of everyday English speech patterns, balancing equal quantities of stress and unstress; and for this reason it makes verse seem to flow naturally. David Mamet, author of memorable screenplays such as *Glengarry Glenross*, has observed that colloquial speech falls naturally into iambic pentameter – if one person begins a ten-beat line, the other will finish it.

STAGE 3: WRITING IN REGULAR RHYTHM

The next stage is to practise writing your own poetry to this rhythm. Consider the following example, where a student writer developed a piece of rhythmic writing from note form:

Field notes/ writer's diary entry

Bus station. Orange lights making everyone look weird. Usual faces for the last bus. That edge in the air – everyone slightly frightened. Girl with zebra pattern purse, squeezing hold of it, huddling up to boyfriend when he arrived.

First rough draft in verse

Once again we're all stuck here, and its late in the orange glow
me, the drunks, the old age pensioners, the girl
with the purse like zebra skin, grabbing hold of it for dear life

Verse draft in iambic metre

and **here** we **are** again be**neath** the **lights**
the **drunk,** the **old,** the **poor** who **have** no **choice**
and **here** again the **girl** who **holds** her **purse**
afraid in **case** it's **robbed**

Take a line of your own poetry, and reorder it to make it into iambic metre. This is intended only as training. Do not expect a masterpiece, only competent rhythmic verse: the equivalent of a musical scale, not a violin solo. Even making competent doggerel will not come easily at first. You will need to reorder some words and discard others when a syllable needs to be added or a stress needs to be dropped, but persevere. You will not always be able to use the word you first thought of, or most wanted. Take heart! Making a pact between sound and sense – rather than simply pursuing your meaning and ignoring sound – is where the craft of poetry begins, and often abandoning your first choice of word for purposes of rhythm will lead you to a better one. When you can do this you will have taken a huge step towards technical proficiency. All other arts of rhythm are built on this basic skill – the ordering of stressed and unstressed syllables.

This sort of exercise – chopping and changing your verse to fit a pre-set rhythm – is not a natural activity and, yes, it will seem awkward at first. But by doing it you will absorb the sound of iambic rhythm until it becomes internalised. Not only will you be able to discipline an irregular line, but you will know at once whether it 'scans' (whether its metre is regular) or not. Thereafter, compose as you will, you will be able to echo this inner beat, just as a motorist can change gear without thinking about it.

STAGE 4: VARYING RHYTHM

To be able to craft a regular metre is a vital skill for the poet – and a useful skill for any writer – but followed as a rule of composition it makes for dull writing. Too much regular rhythm irritates. Pure iambic metre (or any metre sustained with perfect regularity for too long) will begin to sound like a jingle or a ticking clock. For this reason it is comparatively unusual for a poet to write a whole poem – or even a whole line – in purely iambic metre. Sooner or later she will vary her rhythm. This is where a mere technical skill becomes a matter of creative artistry.

First, of course, you must establish a background rhythm which the hearer, or reader, can engage with. Then you begin to adapt it to your own creative purposes. The potential number of these metrical variations and their effects are almost infinite – just as when you have learned to play a guitar, you have almost infinite freedom in composition. Like the musician, however, you will find that composition is best guided by some basic principles of technique and effect.

Stress and attention – the spondee and highlighting meaning

When we stress a syllable it gathers weight and importance. A syllable which bears a stress which is not dictated by the rhythm you have established – that is, which has an 'extra' stress – stands out from the syllables around it. A stressed syllable will, in general, make more impact than an unstressed one. If your background metre is iambic, then adding such an extra stressed syllable will create a double or triple stress. A double stress will lift a word or phrase out of the expected order which you have established, and attract your reader's attention. A unit or foot with two stressed syllables is called a spondee:

lighthouse   cat suit   high heels   programme

Triple stresses are not common in English. When they occur, they stand out even more. Conversely *withholding* an expected stressed syllable (hence creating a double or triple unstress) influences the reader in another way, gliding their attention on until the next stress. (A unit or foot with two unstressed syllables is called *pyrrhic*.) Thus you can direct your reader around the soundscape of your poem, to concentrate their attention where you most want it.

Read aloud and consider the following variations:

1. afraid, she **clutched** her **purse** into her **hand**
   This is iambic metre. Stress is distributed evenly and regularly. It is your starting point.

2. afraid she **clutched** her **purse** in **two hands**
   These are iambic but with variation: a metre is established, but broken by the final spondee. Stress is concentrated in such a way that the girl's hands stand out – they are foregrounded.

3. afraid, she **clutched** her **purse** in **one tight hand**
   Again, this is mostly iambic, but the triple stress places even more emphasis on the image of the hands. Now read aloud and compare

4. afraid, the **zebra** **purse clutched** in her **hand**
   Again, iambic metre forms the background, but attention is shifted to a different image – not just through the redeployment of the adjective, but by the metre. Before the hand was the dominant image; now it is the purse. This effect can be emphasised further:

5. afraid, the **black purse clutched** into her **hand**

> The above exercise demonstrates in microcosm the art of rhythm which you are learning to control. Now take one of your own lines and vary it, play with it, changing the metre to shift emphasis from word to word, image to image. Read it aloud each time. Taste the sense of control over sound which deploying stress *deliberately* gives you. You are on your way.

Concentration of stress draws readers closer to you. Passages of unstressed syllables release their attention. Too much stress and the poem will appear to be shouting. Too little, and the reader will swim their own sweet way out of the spell of your poem; for a poem, like a drop of water, is held together by surface tension: it is not just meaning, but meaning bound tightly by form. That tightness comes from stressed syllables.

Stress and pace – creating mood

Stress – that is, the occurrence of stressed syllables – in general slows down a line. If you want to make your reader linger on a line or phrase, add more stress. If you want to whisk a reader through it, then remove stress. If we take the median point of stress in English poetry as that of iambic metre, which has equal numbers of stressed and unstressed syllables, then an increase in the number of stressed syllables can on occasion add to the solemnity of a line, whereas an increase in the number of unstressed syllables can contribute to a light or comic effect. Bawdy and comic verse often employs more unstressed syllables, for the point is not to meditate on the meaning of the poem, but to come to the joke or comic rhyme. Such verse also tends to have a very strong, obvious rhythm, as the 'tune' it beats out is, as with the limerick, part of the pleasure it yields:

the **sexual life** of the **cam**el is **stranger** than **anyone thinks**

Conversely, the burden of gravity in a subject can be echoed in concentration of stress

Down those **mean streets** a **man must walk** who is **not** himself **mean**

The triple stress that is central to the line hammers home the urgency of the thought. There is, as it were, nowhere to hide, no relaxation at the heart of the line. Try replacing 'a man must walk' with 'a detective is obliged to travel' and you can feel the strength of the line draining away.

I must emphasise that there are no absolute rules for this, and the same metre can be used to generate a variety of effects. The important thing is not to leap to an assumption that such a metre is appropriate to such a subject, but to become more and more aware of how metre works, and how a shift may help you generate the effect you are looking for.

Dactyls

Iambic metre has dominated English poetry; but other rhythms, more noticeable to the ear, can have a marked effect on mood. A ratio of one stress to two unstressed syllables offers different possibilities, and this is the pattern for dactylic verse, or poetry written in dactyls. A dactyl consists of one stressed syllable followed by two unstressed syllables as in:

Wonderful   Violet   Metaphor

Read the following pairs of lines aloud and see what you notice about their respective rhythms:

Emily purchased two bunches of daffodils
Emma bought some flowers

Melanie opened the registered envelope
Mel undid the parcel

I long to escape to the High Pyrenees
I want to go to write in France

Verse which is largely dactylic, such as the first line of each of the pairs in the box above, can embody a fluent, musical melody. It is more like a waltz than a military march: ONE two three ONE two three; not LEFT right LEFT right. Whereas iambic verse 'feels' like normal speech, dactylic verse can seem to 'sing'; that is, it can be used to enhance a number of effects which evoke a lyrical or musical response in the reader. Thomas Hardy uses dactylic metre to accentuate a plaintive, mournful tone:

woman much **missed** how you **call** to me **call** to me

Another effect of this metre can be to provide an echo of the child-like, as it picks up a rhythm popular in nursery rhymes and children's verse. Dactylic lines can occur accidentally in everyday English, but when they do the rhythm tends to be so unusual that we notice something strange or amusing about it. Try this aloud:

Christopher ran to the cinema opening hoping his sister
would entertain everyone.

Anapests

Just as iambic metre has its companion in the trochaic, so dactylic metre has a mirror image in the anapestic. An anapest is a unit of metre which, like the dactyl, has one stressed and two unstressed syllables; but in the anapest the stressed syllable is the first, not the last, of the three. Anapestic metre has the same 'singing' quality and, like dactylic metre, can stir associations with the rhythms of childhood and fairytale.

Edgar Allan Poe, one of the greatest exponents of the hypnotic effects of rhythm, uses largely anapestic metre in his poem 'Annabel Lee'. Note the rhythm yourself, putting this mark \ over an unstressed syllable and this mark X over a stressed syllable.

It was many and many a year ago,

In a kingdom by the sea

That a maiden there lived whom you may know

By the name of ANNABEL LEE

And this maiden she lived with no other thought

Than to love and be loved by me.

Now try writing a few lines of dactylic or anapestic metre. Do not feel you have to follow it exactly, but set out to catch the distinctive music it can embody. Try using it. It is through experimentation and free play (which includes the capacity to write light verse or complete nonsense) that you will deepen your awareness of rhythm.

STAGE 5: MAKING YOUR OWN RHYTHMS

You can follow a rhythm, vary a rhythm and choose between different rhythms. The next stage of your development is the creation of your own rhythms. This ambition is not restricted to poets, but it has a particular relevance to poets. Much poetry today is written in free verse, which has no regular, structured pattern of line length and metre. This does not of course mean that it has no rhythm. To make a poem without a rhythm is like trying to make a drawing without lines. But each line of free verse has its *own* rhythm. This is much harder to do well than following, or varying, an established metrical scheme. Once again, the range of possible permutations – and effects – is endless. But there are some guiding principles. Successful writing of rhythmic prose or free verse depends on two things: maintaining a forward momentum and making a sweet partnership between sound and meaning.

Momentum

The goal of effective writing is the control of your readers, and part of this is control of pace. They must pause where you want them to pause, move on when you want them to be moved on, be jerked to a halt, if necessary, when you wish to ambush or shock them. Partly this will be done through punctuation, and partly it depends on metre.

Stress is the muscle and bone of your writing, be it prose or poetry. Stressed syllables are like the rings along the snake's body – as they clench, they anchor your words, and as they unclench they push them forward. As we have seen, the more stress you put in a line, the slower your reader will move, but this muscular clenching can have other effects also. In prose the more stress you put in, the starker and stronger your style will seem; the less stress you put in, the more conversational and relaxed. Compare the following pairs. In both, line length is one part of the difference, but another is the ratio of stressed to unstressed syllables.

Long ago, when the **last king ruled**, a **man came** from the **North**.

Many winters **ago**, in the **days** of the **emper**or, a **travel**ler **arrived** from the **bor**der.

Consider in particular the effect of the last syllable being stressed or unstressed. The 'tailing off' effect of a final unstress is well known, and is called 'falling' metre in poetry, but it operates in prose also. Once again, neither is of itself better than the other. The important thing is that you are aware of the effects of stress in order to deploy them deliberately.

In poetry there is another factor: the layout of the words on the page, where stress combines with line-breaks to influence pace. Finishing a line with a stress delays the movement through the line-break; finishing with an unstress will move it on more smoothly. Consider the following:

> I long to see you walk
> Lightly towards me

> I long to see you walk lightly
> Towards me

You need not think of whole lines being fast or slow. A single line can effect a transition in pace. In one of the most famous and influential examples of rhythmic prose, stress is gradually increased in frequency, moving from the gentle tempo of storytelling to the enunciation of solemn truth:

> In the be**gin**ning was the **Word**, and the **Word** was **with God,**
> and the **Word was God**

The aural effect of this line, impressive as it is, is based on a simple principle your own prose may easily employ – the increased concentration of stress to match the weight of the subject matter. Thus sound and meaning become one.

Another key way in which stress can enhance sense is in the creation of patterns which link phrases aurally. It is in this context that metre becomes a tool of persuasion. If two phrases share the same metrical form, our ear will sense the connection as an agreement or harmony between them, even though you are unlikely to consciously realise how the link is being made. Advertisers compound the force of this link by adding rhyme, but the underlying structure of a successful slogan depends on its metre, not its rhymes. Often they use a simple device of two parallel phrases which mirror each other metrically, making the phrase memorable and – in a way we are not consciously aware of – satisfying.

> It's the **fish John West** reject that **make John West** the **Best**

> You get a **smart**er in**vest**or at **Alliance** and **Leic**ester

When a metrical pattern is repeated, even in phrases which have no logical link, we hear an apparent progression or association between them. In a less obviously rhetorical way, the matching of the same number of stressed syllables on either side of a pause such as that introduced by a comma creates a sense of order and balance. Note that the number of unstressed syllables in between the stresses need not be exactly the same – the ear is less attuned to them, and sometimes they can even run together without loss of effect. It is the stresses that measure out the beat of the poem:

>I am **Alph**a and **Om**ega, the be**gin**ning and the **end**.

Rhythm can be used to dramatise the tensions and dilemmas within a character's thought:

>I **did not choose** this **fate, nor did I** deny it.

Here the mental balance of a man poised indecisively between two lives is echoed in the balance of two phrases each holding a triple stress followed by a single stress.

STAGE 6: THE BIGGER PICTURE

If your individual lines or sentences are written with a conscious awareness of rhythm, you will find that over the broader sweep of your work certain patterns will recur: sometimes the same, sometimes varied, more like a musical motif in a symphony than the obvious tune of a song.

Your thought has its own rhythms. The way you see the world, its oppositions and harmonies, its tensions and its struggles for resolution, will find an echo in the sound of your work. It must do: for you are now shaping the body of your writing to fit its inner spirit. The patterns of stressed and unstressed syllables which emerge are, like the pattern of ridges and troughs on your thumbprint, beyond your control but unique to you. Rhythm will become part of your voice, and it is your voice that will draw readers back to your work again and again. Equally, your writing will hold echoes of the rhythms which have nourished you. Seek out such nourishment. Listen to recordings of Dylan Thomas's radio drama *Under Milk Wood*, to the infectious beat of rap and dub poetry by Eminem, Benjamin Zephaniah or Linton Kwesi Johnson. Read poetry aloud: the verse of Grace Nichols; the flowing, lyrical rhythms of Seamus Heaney. In prose, try Elizabeth Smart's *By Grand Central Station I Sat Down and Wept*; and contrast it with the tight, hard beat of Hemingway's prose. Seek out the best of rhythmic film dialogue: the slow, elegant courtesy of Ang Lee's southern soldiers in *Ride with the Devil*; the feline repartee of Selina Kyle in *Batman Returns*; the hard-bitten interchanges, resonant single lines and elegiac speeches of *Blade Runner*.

CONCLUSION

R. S. Thomas (1992) speaks of a poem beginning with a tune, a rhythm in the mind. Can you relate his experience to your own composition? When students first begin to study rhythm they often find this idea puzzling or even incredible. Yet just as you may count yourself fluent in another language when you find yourself thinking in it, so it is with rhythm: you may reach the point where you are thinking in sound. At this point, as a new piece of writing rises from its mysterious sources in your mind, it may be the sound – the beat – of the words struggling to find shape that reaches you first. When this happens you are truly making music with words. Learn the art of rhythm and your readers will be captivated. Isn't that the least that your thoughts, your characters, deserve?

5 WRITING POETRY

Gladys Mary Coles

'Poetry is not the thing said but a way of saying it.'

A. E. Housman

WHAT IS POETRY?

Poetry is not only a way of saying but a way of seeing, and an art of suggestion in which language is at its most intense and magical. Poetry is form. Poetry is the shaping of language into special patterns that will bring out more pleasure, more meaning, from the words. A 'poem' without a deliberately chosen form is not a poem; it is a mess of words.

The most important way that poetry is patterned, or formed, is in sound. Poetry is, after all, designed to be read aloud. Fundamental to this patterning is rhythm, and you should read and absorb the lessons of the previous chapter as you begin to compose poetry. The other chief way is rhyme.

Rhyme is intrinsic to the musicality of poetry. It can support mood and meaning, give emphasis, and be an aid to fixing the poem in the memory, as in William Blake's 'The Tyger':

> Tyger! Tyger! burning bright
> In the forests of the night

The traditional way of organising your poem using a pattern of end-rhymes is called a rhyme scheme; letters are used to notate each sound, the letter being repeated each time the same sound is employed, as shown alongside the following quatrain, or four-line verse.

> I have desired to go **a**
> Where springs not fail, **b**
> To fields where flies no sharp and sided hail **b**
> And a few lilies blow. **a**
> *Gerard Manley Hopkins, 'Heaven-Haven'*

Full rhyme

Ballads, and songs generally, use full rhymes – repetition of all the final sound of the words, as in sound/bound, cross/moss, arts/parts. Full rhyme needs to be handled with subtlety and care, or it will seem too heavy: in particular, you must avoid the impression of a line being *rhyme driven* – that is, the sense twisted to fit the rhyme, rather than the rhyme appearing to be a natural expression of the sense. Good rhyming is unobtrusive. Try to pair words which have an element of surprise. The English language is not rich in full rhymes, and overuse has made many combinations sound hackneyed – for example, trees/breeze, night/bright. Full rhyme can be satisfying, however, in humorous and satiric verse (like the limerick), or in work where the sense of the speaking – or singing – voice is strong, as in rap lyrics, which often use couplets (two-line stanzas) with an aa bb cc rhyme scheme. The songs of Eminem and the poetry of Benjamin Zephaniah both give powerful examples of such hard, definite full rhymes, but both also use alternately flowing and broken rhythms to spring surprises on the ear, rhyming, for example, *black* against the first syllable of *accent*.

Half-rhyme

Apart from those who write poetry for – or drawn from the tradition of – live performance, poets today tend to use subtler forms than full rhyme. Half-rhyme is when two rhyming words have different vowel sounds but identical final consonants: kill/sell, most/mast. It is a subtle sound technique, giving greater flexibility than full rhyme, and effective in imbuing a poem with emotional undertones and resonance. Wilfred Owen used half-rhyme as end-rhyme systematically in his war poetry to create a sense of disturbance, as, for example, in ground/grind; loads/lids/lads; hall/Hell. Consider the effect of such discords in his poem, 'Strange Meeting':

> I am the enemy you killed, my friend.
> I knew you in this dark: for so you frowned
> Yesterday through me as you jabbed and killed.
> I parried; but my hands were loath and cold.

Owen made lists of para-rhymes in preparation for writing poems. Such pairings train the ear and can help you at a subconscious level.

Rhymes in action

Choose two rhyme schemes from poems you have read, and compose two poems using each scheme. Create your own rhyme schemes, using both full rhymes and half-rhymes. Be consistent, sustaining your scheme all through the poem.

Internal rhyme

Rhyming (or half-rhyming) words need not occur in the most obvious position, at the end of a line. They can be placed anywhere *within* the line or lines of a poem, creating an echo or chime. They also have binding power, giving the poem a sense of unity and cohesion, which is useful in free verse (see below). For example:

> he loved her like that, her black gloves in the rain
> tight boots for nightclubs, the pain she left him

Here love and glove, tight and night, rhyme in a way subtle enough to set up an echo without drawing attention to themselves as they would at the end of the line. Pain and rain make a more distant relationship between the two lines, but still illustrate the way threads of sound can give the ear pleasure, and help orient your reader towards the threads of meaning from which you weave a poem. As an example of the marvellously rich possibilities of rhyme, read aloud Selima Hill's intricately worked sonnet 'The Hare'.

THE SONNET

The sonnet is the most popular of the traditional forms. With fourteen lines of iambic pentameter (see Chapter 4), it combines brevity with depth, and is versatile in its capacity to debate many subjects beyond the traditional ones of love, death and transience. While its roots are in the Renaissance and beyond, the sonnet is still used by contemporary writers from Jackie Kay to Mimi Khalvati. The Italian derivation of the name, 'little song', suggests its lyrical quality. The now less frequently used Petrarchan or Italian sonnet has an **abba cddc cdecde** rhyme scheme. The more popular Shakespearean or English sonnet involves only five rhymes instead of seven. Organised into three quatrains and a closing couplet, its rhyme scheme is **abab cdcd efef gg**. It often builds a thought or argument in three separate stages through its three quatrains, and then resolves it in the last two lines, the rhyming couplet having a clinching effect, often being an epigrammatic summing up, as in Shakespeare's Sonnet XCIV:

> For sweetest things turn sourest by their deeds;
> Lilies that fester smell far worse than weeds.

Poets first attempting a sonnet sometimes feel constrained by the strong scheme of end-rhymes to write a poem of fourteen end-stopped lines, each one almost self-contained, and stopping at the rhyme, but this can lead to a stilted effect. Try *enjambment* (from the French for 'to step over'), running your sense on through the line-break into the next line, as here:

Devon Churches
you keep looking for it, a place so still
that after the door's echo you can hear
a lark, a tractor fields away, aisles filled
with the cold quiet shock of others' prayer:
that pause. The saints in the late August
sun bleeding scarlet stains across the face
of an unplastered wall, the lingering hush
of dying lilies. As though some other place
were near, held between breaths, as in the glass,
Adam is held in the red clench of scales;
as though in the damp book you'd find, at last
a cryptic hint of some elusive grail,
the confirmation of this search: some guide,
some word or name, a sign you recognise.

Edmund Cusick

None of these lines except the last one ends with a full stop, but lines 4 and 10 are nonetheless end-stopped: that is, the sense comes to a pause with the line-break. Such pauses serve to slow the poem down; whereas the enjambment at the end of lines 2 and 5, for example, serve to drive the poem on.

SYLLABICS

Some poems are structured not according to the number of stressed syllables, but according to the number of all the syllables. The best known of these forms is the three-line Japanese *haiku*. It has seventeen syllables, the first line having five, the second line seven, the third five. The spirit of this form lies in the intense perception (traditionally of nature, the seasons and the universe) caught in a single image:

In the dawn a pale
leaf trembles before the sun
light steals its shadow.

Haiku is a discipline both of words and of the mind that creates it. Try this form and see how it imposes stillness, making you search for the heart of any moment and its meaning.

FREE VERSE

Each free verse poem you write has its own structure, designed and shaped individually. The key controlling factor is the line-break. With practice you will learn intuitively to shape your lines – to lineate – for flow, surprise and emphasis. You need to be aware exactly where and why you are ending a line and beginning a new one; otherwise your poem will seem mere chopped-up prose. The purpose of a line-break is often to sustain tension and interest, using the last word on your line as a springboard to the next, making your reader want to read on. Do not let your line sag at the end with 'a', 'the' or a weak preposition, such as 'for', 'with' or 'by'. For example, compare

> He came, with a basket of gifts, fish for
> the women to cook

with

> He came, with a basket of gifts, fish
> for the women to cook

and you will see that the first line ends limply, and was strengthened by rearrangement.

If you are *end-stopping*, the pause at the end of the line must, like all your technical decisions, be for a good reason: perhaps a comma indicating the natural breathing pause between phrases (you will hear this by reading your work aloud), or a full stop ending a sentence or phrase and giving a sense of completion before the poem moves on. Do not end-stop too often as it kills flow. Use enjambment, flowing from one line to the next, even perhaps from one stanza to the next.

Line-breaks

Consider these lines from the poem 'Across the Berwyns', written out as prose:

> Snowfall slither. A warning on the sign at the bottom of the B road climb. I'm seeking the ice plateau, need, after fire, the salving of snowscapes, white silence.

Write them out as poetry, choosing where to make line-breaks. Some hints: the poet chose to bring in an element of danger in the first line. Can you hear a half-rhyme? The poet used it as a binding device between two lines presenting danger.

When you have done this, try taking a poem in free form and writing it out without its line-breaks, as prose. Then write the poem out again, placing line-breaks where you think they should be. Compare your version with the original. You will now have two poems, similar, but not identical in the meanings which they create. Think about the different effects the different line-breaks make. Then take one of your own poems and try the same exercise.

PUNCTUATION

Move too slowly in a poem and you will bore the reader; move too quickly and they will be confused, or miss your more subtle points. The speed of a poem is controlled in part by its line-breaks and its metre, but also by its punctuation. A comma indicates a slight pause. The full stop indicates a longer pause. The semi-colon and colon are somewhere in between the two. The decision of how many sentences to divide your poem into – how many full stops to use – can be crucial in its effect on your readers, even though it is one which happens unconsciously, without the reader knowing how they are being directed.

Judging your speed

Copy a poem you enjoy, and delete its punctuation. Then repunctuate it yourself. Read the two poems aloud, and see if you can judge why the poet made the decisions that she did. Try varying the punctuation in your own poems, and judging the effects.

IMAGERY

Learn to think and feel through images: through elements of sensory experience which can be vividly real to a reader, yet which can quietly carry more symbolic or intuitive meaning than the physical description alone. There is a sense in which all poetry seeks epiphany – the single telling image which unfolds or reveals a deeper sense of how the world is. Be physical: give your readers concrete words (dog, onion, munch, granite, howl) rather than abstract ones (hope, heartbreak, love, beauty). Be detailed: give them 'apples' or 'birches' not 'fruit' or 'trees'. Study the way that feelings are always incarnated in and known through the flesh: read Sharon Olds and Vicki Feaver, Ann Gray and Ted Hughes for exemplary evocations of felt, tactile reality; John Burnside and Pauline Stainer for a sense of how that physical reality can mediate other realms, lifting the epiphanic into the sacramental.

Through images, you should not need the abstract word 'beauty'; rather your challenge is to show the reader *in what way* something is beautiful. Poets draw down other images also, at the level of imagination rather than description: the object is not 'physically' present in the poem's subject, but is evoked to make the subject more real. Among these are similes: they make an imaginative link between two things, but keep them separate through the use of the prepositions 'like' or 'as'. Similes thread common speech in expressions such as 'wet as an otter's pocket', but poets seek out their own, original similes: for example, Kathleen Jamie's image of being held 'like a man at a deck-rail in a gale'.

Students wishing to extend the range of their similes can drink deep of the work of Selima Hill, whose idiom of startling similes rises to surreal and fantastical heights; but even in their baroque or absurd glory, they too are always anchored in physical reality.

Other images can be termed metaphors: they do not merely describe a thing, but unite the apparent subject with another object, collapsing the distance between the two things compared. It is in this transformation that the power of metaphor lies. In 'Daddy', Sylvia Plath refers to her father as *a black shoe/In which I have lived like a foot/For thirty years*, a metaphor which encloses a simile.

Images within a poem will gain greater power if they connect. A poem reverberates by means of a pattern of images which refract each other and interrelate. In my poem 'As Mad As a Hatter's Child', various images of roundness (bowler hats, barrels, horses' flanks, men's stomachs, bonnets) reflect the key image of pregnancy and also evoke the nineteenth-century world of this poem with its theme of the deaths of hatters' babies and young children.

Lists

Write a poem based on a list. Choose a subject which fascinates or repels you, and make a list of things you associate with it. Make those things as tangible, as concrete as possible, and you will be surprised at how their emotional or imaginative significance shines through. For one possible example look at Carole Satyamurti's poem 'Mouthfuls', which focuses in sensory detail on the types of sweets enjoyed in childhood, such as sherbet lemons: 'vicious yellow' whose 'sugar splinters lacerate'.

TITLES

are an intrinsic part of your poems, not labels. They should not only be apposite, but used to hint at the content, create expectation. They can set the tone and/or give important information, such as indications of the poem's place and period. In some cases the title acts as the first line, as in

Leafburners
move quietly as smoke

An untitled poem is a lost opportunity, and gives the impression of a failure of inspiration, or a lazy poet.

Titling

Read the contents page of a poetry anthology. Write down all the titles which make you want to read a poem, and all those that definitely make you want to avoid one! What makes the good ones effective? Look back at your own titles. Try a few alternatives for the same poem, and see what response you get from your readers.

FIRST LINES, FIRST DRAFTS

As you begin to compose your poem, do not worry too much about the first words. The process is like uncorking a bottle of wine – the hardest bit is getting it moving. Let your poem flow – the first line might well be one which you edit out eventually, but you need to write it to get started. The main consideration is to keep going until you have run out of 'inspiration'. Always read your poems aloud as you are drafting them, and your rhythm will stay strong. Get a first draft down, and then work at it, shaping words as a sculptor shapes clay or marble, gradually growing closer to the form she desires.

All sorts of language can find expression in poetry – but *never* use words because you think they sound poetic. The worst examples are old-fashioned phrases: 'thees', 'thous' and other archaisms, and poeticisms such as 'wondrous', 'morn', and 'blest'. Such language even at its best sounds out of date; at its worst it will make your poem seem clichéd and insincere, because its words are not your own.

REVISIONS

Most poets find that poems take time to grow, and pass though several drafts before they are finished, sometimes with weeks or months between drafts. Allow the form to evolve from the subject or theme at the heart of the poem, rather than imposing a form upon it. The first verse form you try may not be the best. While a stanza can be of any length, that length should constitute a kind of paragraphing, each new stanza forwarding the movement of the poem. One line, or even a single word or phrase, can constitute a stanza, but these will need to carry some special importance. Setting a line off by the white space around it draws attention to that line, and this too needs to be justified. Read Tom Leonard and Peter Finch to get you thinking of new ways to use the space of a white page.

Cut superfluous adjectives and adverbs. Sometimes condensing can be achieved by eliminating prosy words; and conjunctions such as 'and':

then she took the spoon from me and licked it slowly

becoming

she took the spoon, licked it slowly

Prune your draft, aiming always to identify the heart of the poem – the significant detail, the telling image – and to cut the lines where you labour points or explain yourself. In all your reading, appreciate how much the poets you love *do not* say; how much they trust you to make the links they prompt, not feeling they must spell out their meaning, but offering it to be discovered by the right readers. Read poets whose editing genius makes whole worlds out of the fewest of words: George MacKay Brown, Emily Dickinson, Moniza Alvi.

VOICE

As you build up a body of poetry, your poetic character, your rhythms and unique perspectives will begin to resonate. This is your *poetic voice*. You can hear it in poets from Jeni Couzyn to Grace Nichols, Robert Graves to Amelia Blossom Pegram, W. B. Yeats to Michèle Roberts. You will recognise it when you hear it, for it carries the authority of what is known through the poet's whole being – whatever the poetic persona adopted – not what is assumed or pretended for effect. You will learn to hear false notes also, in others' work and in your own. The search for voice, in both your reading and writing, is simply the pain, and liberation, of honesty. The sureness of your own voice – which your readers will recognise before you do – is a sign of growing maturity as a poet. Paradoxically, the confidence in your own identity may be the springboard for you to step out of an autobiographical range, and write poems which explore other characters' experiences, from their point of view, and in their language.

THE DRAMATIC MONOLOGUE

is a poem told from the point of view of a specific character, often drawn from history or myth. For examples, look at the work of U. A. Fanthorpe, Liz Lochhead and Carol Ann Duffy; and for further thoughts on this option read the relevant section in Chapter 8, 'Writing for stage'. Dramatic monologues can be inspired by paintings as well as books. *The Poet's View: Poems for Paintings in the Walker Art Gallery* offers many examples (Coles, 1996).

Stepping out

Write a poem in the voice of a figure from history or myth. Speak from a particular moment in their lives. Boost your imagination by research, but only let it emerge as and when it seems natural.

ENDING

When is a poem finished? When you have the core of its meaning, and when the whole is technically competent, particularly in terms of rhythm. In your final revision it may be the closing lines of your poem, or the opening ones, the 'getting there' and the 'concluding moral' that can be cut, letting the experience speak for itself. Remember the power of restraint and understatement. Write poems which trust their readers, which imagine alert, perceptive, knowledgeable readers, and such readers will find you.

ADVANCING AS A POET

No one ever became a poet without constantly reading poetry. Read every day. Read omnivorously until you find the poets who excite you. It can be helpful to start with anthologies: historical ones such as the Norton and Oxford anthologies of English verse, and contemporary ones that line the shelves of any good bookshop. Poets talk to each other through their work, and it is through the poems of this month, this year, that the great conversation that is poetry advances. Get hold of the latest issues of poetry magazines, and you will become part of that conversation, if only as a listener at first. Seize every chance to attend live poetry readings. Keep reading, keep writing. Poetry is a vocation, and once you follow it, you may find there is no going back.

6 SHORT STORY WRITING

Jenny Newman

INTRODUCTION

The short story is the best place to start writing fiction. It can be long enough to let you build character, write dialogue, experiment with plot, and in general flex your writing muscles; but it need not be so long that you get bogged down. Because of its brevity and precision, the short story gives you invaluable training in the skill of editing. You may, if you wish, redraft it from start to finish, polish it, and bring all your talent to bear on it, and not lose touch with your initial impulse. As V. S. Pritchett (2001) says, 'The novel tends to tell us everything, whereas the short story tells us only one thing, and that intensely.'

Though the short story's roots are in the fairytales, moral fables, folktales and ghost stories our ancestors told round the fire, its descendants are just as at home in the age of 'sudden fiction' and the sound bite. People's first response to a crisis is often to reshape it as a story. It is the art of the present moment, a snapshot rather than a biography. The writer does not need to spell out what happened before, or what will happen next. Instead, she learns to select those images and details which will resonate in the mind of her reader or listener, and make him feel he knows all he needs to know about characters and setting.

The short story writer depends on what Raymond Carver (1986) calls 'a unique and exact way of looking at things, and [on] finding the right context for expressing that way of looking'. This is the ideal form in which to begin uncovering your writer's voice: that slant on experience and way of describing it that will distinguish your work from everyone else's.

BEGINNING

The blank page is often daunting, and the best advice is to start your first story anywhere you can. See Chapter 1, 'The writer's notebook', on how to avoid wasting precious writing time struggling to dredge up ideas. Your inspiration may be an image hoarded against a rainy day, or the pulse of an idea which lodges itself in your imagination and insists you develop it. Whatever your starting point, commit it to paper as soon as you can.

Any first paragraph that engages your reader is a success. Any other is a failure. If your beginning seems inert, remember that you can always cut it, and start at a point which foreshadows a future conflict. Enter the first scene as late you can without being baffling, and plant a 'hook' or attention grabber. This could be a question, implicit or explicit, which the rest of the story will answer. Help your reader picture the setting with some 'weather in the streets'; but do not load her with information, or insert long flashbacks which distract her from the narrative present.

Titles

Take time choosing a good title, because it is probably what will strike your reader first. Your title may, for instance, be

- the name of the central character;
- an object of significance to the plot;
- an indication of its theme;
- a sentence or phrase which tells part of the story;
- a key to reading the story, as in Michael Carson's 'All over the place' (Minshull, 1994).

CHARACTER

Frank O'Connor (1963) believes that the short story is the province of what he calls 'submerged population groups' such as 'tramps, artists, lonely idealists, dreamers and spoilt priests'. Even if you do not know such people, keep an eye open for those who live at odds with the so-called mainstream. Adapted to the demands of your plot, their imagined insights may well fuel a story. Traditional tales often describe a magical or out-of-the-way episode, and many modern short story writers treasure this link with what is uncanny or bizarre. Writing from a divergent perspective is part of what the French novelist Albert Camus called 'defamiliarisation', or making the ordinary look strange, and can be seen as the short story's – as opposed to the novel's – distinguishing characteristic.

Modern readers can grow bored with description, so introduce your story people economically and memorably. It is more entertaining to reveal a character through the way he or she drives, smokes, or reads the paper than by resorting to tired descriptions of eye colour. Dialogue, action, dress and physiognomy can all be pressed into service. Learn to be precise. If you write, 'Melvyn climbed down from his shiny black four wheel drive', your reader will learn more than from, 'Melvyn got out of his car.' Consider inventing a main character who is different from you in, say, background, class or gender. This may help you to find a voice which differs from your everyday tone, and thus make your writing more distinctive.

Your main character can be central to the action, or else confined to the sidelines. There are many successful examples of overlooked or impotent central characters, such as the paralysed man bullied in an expensive restaurant in Rose Tremain's 'My Wife is a White Russian'; but it may be easier to start with a protagonist who initiates the action.

As the resolution will depend on a change taking place, choose a main character who is capable of a realisation or transformation which, however small, can be shown to be crucial. Intimate at least the shadow of that change by the end of your first page.

Character building

- Write a page describing your main character. Even if it does not all find its way into the finished story, it is this 'underwater' knowledge which lends conviction to the details you select.
- When describing appearance, do not linger on what is predictable, but find a feature which sticks out from the norm, or hints at a hidden trait, or spells insight or disaster. 'Celia Jones had a face like the blade of an axe.' What does this mean for the plot? How does it point to the end of your story?
- Your reader will take at most half an hour to read or listen to your story, and usually less, so keep your cast to a maximum (excluding walk-on roles) of three or four.

POINT OF VIEW

Point of view is a literary term for the lens through which your reader looks at the world you create. Your basic choice is between a *character–narrator* and *writing in the third person*. (Technically, if you choose the latter, you will be writing as an author–narrator, not a character–narrator.)

Character–narrator

If one of your characters is telling the story, you are committed to writing in either the first person or, very unusually, the second person.

First-person character–narrator

> My mother says I take after my dad, not her. I was a scally at school, sagging regularly, and bent on leaving as soon as I could to earn the money to buy myself a good time – a good time being pubbing and clubbing.
>
> Evans (1994)

This is a good choice for beginners, because it locates your reader firmly in the mind of one character. Many famous writers continue to exploit this voice because of what Graham Swift calls its located, ground-level view. Its success depends on your ability to find a convincing voice and stick to it, cutting any flourishes which take us outside your character–narrator's head.

Despite its popularity, this method has drawbacks. It is tricky to end with the death of a first-person narrator. Also, it is a difficult mode in which to tell your reader more than your narrator might reasonably know. This can be uncomfortably limiting if, say, your narrator is a child, which may be why so many stories about young children are written in the third person. More crucially, it is hard to describe your narrator's appearance, or a change of expression. There are ways of overcoming this handicap: another character may comment on your narrator's looks; or else you can resort to the traditional method of having her look in the mirror.

Second-person character–narrator

> You shrugged off your dress without closing the curtains, and let it slither to the floor. Wearing only your silk cami-knickers, you flopped on my bed and took a last swig of Monbazillac. Then you passed out with your Benson & Hedges still burning.

Although its rarity lends freshness, this is a difficult voice through which to structure a story. In Jamaica Kincaid's 'Girl', for instance, the story's introduction, climax and resolution are all created through the rhetoric of the mother–speaker, as is the character of the daughter whom she is haranguing. This challenging form is close to the dramatic monologue, more fully discussed in Chapter 8, 'Writing for stage'.

Third person

Though there are many variants of this mode, your basic choice is between:

* limited point of view
* omniscience
* objectivity.

Third-person *limited* point of view

> He had his theme. But whenever he sat down at the word-processor the facility which had once made writing a pleasure – and brought him a brief notoriety – eluded him, evanescing like the smoke from the illicit cigarettes he lit one after another and leaving him with a sour mouth and pulsing head.
>
> Evans (1988)

Like the first person, this narrative method is popular for its tight focus. It does, however, give you a little more freedom. If you are skilled, it is possible to speak, as it were, over your point-of-view character's head. In James Joyce's 'Clay' the reader, unlike the gullible laundry worker Maria, knows that the man on the bus is a thief and (helped by the story's title) that the soft wet substance that Maria touches is garden clay. The title also helps in Graham Greene's 'I Spy' (1970), where, unlike the twelve-year-old, we realise that his father has been spying for the Germans. This story also demonstrates another advantage of the third-person limited viewpoint: you can draw back far enough to describe how your point-of-view character looks, what he is wearing, or a change in his appearance, without sabotaging your perspective.

Third-person *omniscient* (all-knowing) narrator

This is for when you wish to extend your range.

> There is nothing of consequence in a red balloon but the six-year-old heiress, Grace Cooper Glass, marvels at it, open-mouthed, and forgets to even breathe. She is charmed that something so round and fatly red can fly, and Master Milltown Blake is charmed by her. She is so young, so plump, so volatile.
>
> In the lives that are to come, each will remember this moment, slight though it is: the red balloon, Washington Square, the spring day's petal sheen. They will record it, recreate it time and again in letters, diaries, poetry and prose. They will be the most important person in each other's lives. They will anchor one another.
>
> Friel (2000)

As omniscient narrator you may inhabit the mind of any character you wish, describe their pasts and predict their futures, and interpret their feelings. You may also direct the reader explicitly, or communicate what you see as truths or matters of principle; but be sparing with your facts and observations, because few modern readers like to be lectured. If you exhort them too much, or they feel you are showing off at their expense, they may grow alienated, and stop reading.

There are many degrees of omniscience. You may, if you wish, restrict yourself to two or three characters, or nip into one mind only briefly, or throw your reader no more than an occasional comment. Feel free to experiment, and decides which role suits you best. But remember that, like changing lanes on the motorway, it is dangerous to switch viewpoints at random. Your reader can become confused and unsettled.

Third-person *objective* point of view

> The store detective's nose twitched. 'So this silk blouse fell into your shopping bag? Complete with hanger and price-tag?'
>
> The woman's shoes were down-at-heel and her calves blotched with chilblains. 'Yes,' she said. 'I think it must have done.'
>
> 'That's very likely.' The detective's fish-eyes turned flat. 'Now let's see what the Manager has to say.'

Here the narrator stays outside every character's point of view, and confines herself to noting what anyone in their vicinity might observe. A famous exponent of this form is Ernest Hemingway, who in stories such as 'Hills Like White Elephants' gives his readers the data to know his characters better than they know themselves. The pleasure of this mode is that it often makes the reader feel astute. The snag is that it can feel a little cold, with so much hinging on the gap between what characters do and what they say, and with their feelings deduced rather than explored.

When you establish a point of view at the start of a story, you implicitly invite the reader to enter into a contract: this is the way that together we will see the world. If that contract is broken, you risk losing your reader. For any voice to be convincing, you must abide by its limitations, and devise ways where necessary to overcome them.

Childhood memory

- Write down a memory from the years before you were ten. It could relate to your first day at school, the death of a pet: anything you like, no matter how small, as long as it aroused deep feeling. Write freely, not letting the nib of your pen leave the page. Try and inhabit the child that you were then, and remember to use all your senses: the size of desks and chairs, the smell of a nappy, your first close look at Santa Claus, or the feeling of a bird's feathers.
- Wait a day, then rewrite the episode in the first person from the point of view of someone else involved, such as a parent or schoolmate. They need not have played a major part in your first account. Get inside their head and stay there, remembering that a shift of viewpoint can alter the plot (an event which is important to one person may be insignificant to another).

> Experiment with all points of view, or try writing in a different tense, then compare your two versions. What are their strengths and weaknesses?

DIALOGUE

Good dialogue is a great enlivener which develops character and propels plot. It can also vary pacing, deftly reveal your characters' incomes, jobs, geographical region, and class, and lend texture to your prose style. The first rule of good dialogue is to use it.

The second rule is not to confuse it with everyday speech. Realism is a literary convention – or set of conventions – and its dialogue works harder than every day talk. Avoid exchanges which in real life would express nothing more than a general sociability (this speech mode is sometimes known as the phatic). Be sparing with adverbs (such as 'loudly') attached to speech tags (such as 'he said'). If you must mention volume, for example, it is better to use a verb like 'bellow'. In general it is wise to stick to the almost invisible he said/she said, because a lot of different tags – replied, commented, averred, called, shouted – distract the reader. The most elegant solution is to dispense with speech tags where it is possible without sacrificing clarity. As long as you move to a fresh line with each change of speaker, and give every character their own speech pattern, you can expect your reader to do some work.

Though dialogue can drive the action, it should never be laden with exposition ('The bomb will go off at midnight. Unless we can find the special six-inch spanner, the Cameron house will be blown sky high'). If you want to use dialogue as a way of conveying information to the reader, either the speaker must need to say it, or the listener need to hear it, and preferably both. Avoid smart-alec repartee, student banter, and showing off at the reader's expense. Keep a short story collection near your desk for a range of examples of dialogue correctly laid out and punctuated.

Write a quarrel scene

Strong dialogue often conveys a character's will indirectly. Write a conversation between two men of different ages who are disagreeing about something minor: say, the merits of tea bags vs. leaf tea. The discord between them goes deeper than that. Make sure that your reader will sense at least part of it.

PLOT

Because the short story lends itself to experimentation, there are many ways of approaching plot. In a recent newspaper article Jane Smiley described playing her creative writing students the first movement of Mozart's C major quintet. When it was over she said to them, 'Now you know all there is to know about writing a story.' She wanted her students' work to reproduce the 'tension between the desire to linger over the beautiful harmonies between the instruments, the equivalent of words, and the longing for the music to go forward, the equivalent of the storyline.'

Raymond Carver (1986) also identifies tension as a key element, but for him it comes from 'a sense that something is imminent, that certain things are in relentless motion'. Keep the timescale tight and do not overload your story with events. Though the novel's narrative task is amplification, the short story's is restraint, and its plot can be described as the process by which you build up to the single incident or insight you wish to resonate in your reader's mind. Do not distract her by unnecessary scene-shifting.

Short stories are now more diverse than at any other point in their history. In your search for suitable structures, read the work of your favourite contemporaries, jot down their plots in your writer's journal, and adapt them to your own purposes. In 'All over the place', for example, Michael Carson gives us 30 years of his heroine's life through the flotsam of her travels, which include a scrawl in an exercise book, a banker's draft, lines in a baptismal register, graffiti, and an inscription on an agate pendant. Michèle Roberts' 'Une Glossaire/A Glossary' is a list of descriptions of people, places, food, furniture, clothes and events. Suniti Namjoshi reworks fables, Salman Rushdie rewrites Urdu tales, and Emma Tennant updates classical legends (for more ideas on this subject, consult Chapter 3, 'Working with myth'). Some stories may be less a chain of events, and more a process of discovering where an image or sentence fits. Liam O'Flaherty's 'The Flood', for example, can be seen as a deepening of meaning by way of description. A plot may even, as Joyce Carol Oates (1994) points out, 'be wholly interior, seemingly static, a matter of the progression of a character's thought'. Though all plots need to develop and resolve themselves, in stories by writers such as Gertrude Stein and Samuel Beckett it is often language itself that metamorphoses. But remember that if you jettison recognisable characters and sharply dramatised scenes you will lose some readers who believe that character is plot, and plot character.

Experiment with structure

Take a headline that intrigues you – say, IGUANA LOST IN CITY
PARK. From whose point of view will you tell the story: the owner's,
the iguana's, a terrified park-keeper's or a predatory taxidermist's?
Will the tone be surreal, tense, descriptive or meditative? What is the
story really about, and what has changed by the end?

What to do if you are stuck for a plot

For Aristotle successful plots have a beginning, which introduces
conflict, a middle section which develops it, and an ending which
resolves it.

If you feel at a loss, read the section on plot in Chapter 14, 'Writing
for children', and remember that however small the thing your character desires, it must be important to her, as this gives value to her
actions. If your heroine fails to come alive, try pushing her desire to an
extreme. Then you will have the start of a plot. The questions you ask
yourself about her motives will strengthen the portrait as your story
unfolds.

In your early attempts at the short story it is safest to choose an antagonist who gives you scope for dialogue and interaction – two excellent
'hooks'. If you give him some of the best lines, your fiction will not
become propaganda.

The antagonist does not always have to be human. Your hero may be
thwarted by the weather, or sexual attraction, or by timorousness and
gentility, as in Katherine Mansfield's 'The Daughters of the Late Colonel';
or he could be up against a puzzle, like Edgar Allan Poe's detective in
'Murders in the Rue Morgue'. In all such situations you can develop the
kind of conflict which typifies many of the best stories from *The Iliad* to
ET. It is better to focus on small disagreements, and let them be keenly
felt, than to snatch at a huge issue and fail to develop it. For examples of
momentous tales which hinge on minor events, read any short story by
Chekhov or Carver.

It is your job to make life hard for your characters at least some of the
time, so be sure they do not get what they want straightaway. Dramatise
the obstacles, which are traditionally three in number. One setback
shows the antagonist's power, the second builds tension and the third
forms the story's climax. When you invent your setbacks, remember Jack
Bickham's warning (1994): a character's dose of flu or cancelled train may
serve to heighten our sympathy, but bad luck is no substitute for 'give
and take, manoeuvre, struggle and tension'.

ENDING

Although many talented writers have ignored or subverted the above guidelines, followed with flair they provide a reliable way of producing a readable story with a choice of four basic endings: the protagonist gets what she wants and lives happily ever after, or realises that her goal was not worth having; or she does not get what she wants, and it ruins her life; or else she sees she was better off without whatever it had been in the first place.

There are, however, many other ways of writing a conclusion. Whichever one you choose, remember that it is your story's strongest statement, and because of the form's brevity it should in some way be contained in its beginning, like Ouroboros, the snake with its tail in its mouth. If your opening paragraphs lack direction, the resolution will probably be blurred, and your reader will feel cheated.

The twist in the tail, made famous by the American, O. Henry, has gone out of fashion; but do not despise the revelation which can illuminate a whole story retrospectively, as in the last line of dialogue in Rudyard Kipling's 'The Gardener'. Instead of rising to a climax, many modern stories confine themselves to an acute realisation in the mind of the central character: which Joyce defined as an epiphany, or moment of vision, as in the closing lines of his 'Araby'.

Joyce Carol Oates (1994) believes that you need not end with a spelt-out statement, as long as you signal 'a tangible change of some sort; a distinct shift in consciousness, a deepening of insight'. Today that change, she believes, can be confined to the reader's consciousness. Either way, make sure a change or a realisation takes place, because without it there can be no story.

7 WRITING FOR SCREEN AND TELEVISION

Dave Jackson

INTRODUCTION

Screenwriting reaches millions of people every day. There will always be a demand for writers with the skill to tell stories economically and visually. Although most people think of Hollywood as the ultimate goal for screenwriters, British film and television currently offer considerable opportunities.

Screenplays are plans for proposed films or television programmes. They are not self-contained pieces of creative writing like poems or novels. They are like blueprints for buildings yet to be constructed, and their purpose lies beyond the words on the page. They are only the first stage of a collaborative process with producers, directors and actors.

A screenplay may go through many changes and will remain *work in progress* until the film is finished. Films can cost enormous sums of money to produce and the chances of a screenwriter's original vision surviving intact are slim. Perhaps this is why many successful screenwriters like Woody Allen, Jane Campion, Quentin Tarantino, Mike Leigh and Kevin Smith choose to direct their own work.

This is not meant to put you off screenwriting. William Goldman (1984) urges aspiring screenwriters to find outlets such as poetry and novel writing for the creative urges that screenwriting will not satisfy; but he also points out that for his first two novels he was paid $7,500, while for his first Hollywood script he received $80,000. The point is that screenwriting can have more to do with making money than it has to do with producing *art*. It is one of the few areas of creative writing where you stand a chance of making a reasonable living, and there is always the possibility of striking it rich.

If this appeals, it is important to get a feel for your chosen craft. Watch and analyse as much film and television drama as you can, and read lots of screenplays. Many successful and unsuccessful screenwriters have written books on screenwriting. Most of them are American, and offer what may seem like formulaic approaches. While varying in some respects, they tend to agree on certain basic principles:

* A screenplay is a story told in pictures.
* Screenplays need structure.
* Screenplays deal with a central protagonist (sometimes a pair, or less often a group).
* A screenplay's ending dictates its beginning.

You may think this sounds restrictive, and prefer to ignore the 'rules' and adopt a more intuitive approach. Beware. Though you may be successful, it is more likely that you will make your task more difficult. You should at least have an understanding of what you are rejecting. Everyone in the film industry has absorbed these rules and will ask questions such as, 'What is your inciting incident?' If you do not know what they are talking about, they may assume you do not know anything about screenwriting.

What follows is a summary of some generally accepted principles of writing feature films, some related writing exercises, and a short guide to screenplay layout. This will be followed by a briefer discussion of television writing, how it differs from cinema, and a short guide to its various forms. For a more detailed discussion of what makes a good screenplay, you should consult some of the many books on the subject. Each writer has his or her own angle, and it is worth considering as many perspectives as possible.

VISUALISATION

Novels can deal with a character's inner life, explain their thoughts and feelings and detail their memories. Syd Field (1982) stresses that a screenplay is a story told in pictures. You must learn to think visually. Forget about dialogue for now. Dialogue comes last. Think instead about the ways in which films *show* rather than *tell* a story. Think about the openings you like. How do they introduce you to their central characters and the worlds they inhabit?

Many films tell us a lot about a character, their world and their situation before a word is spoken, by opening with an establishing shot of the character's environment: the New York skyline, for instance, or a planet seen from space.

East is East opens with a Christian parade through the terraced streets of a northern English town. The participants' clothing indicates that the film is set in the 1970s. Amongst the white marchers are a group of young Asians laughing and carrying banners. Suddenly they panic. Their Muslim father has come out to watch the parade. They veer off down alleys to avoid being seen, rejoining the parade only after it has passed him. This sets up the location, introduces the main characters, and tells us the central conflict of the film, the clash between the father's values and his children's. We receive most of this information visually.

Many films use colour and visual metaphor to convey information. In David Lynch's *Blue Velvet*, red and yellow flowers and a white picket fence against a too-blue sky introduce a suburban paradise, a palette of primary colours. A man waters his garden. But in darkness, beneath the grass, carnivorous insects engage in violent struggle. The hose becomes twisted, pressure builds. Suddenly the man has a stroke. Paradise is disturbed. The first time we see Jeffery, the central character, he is in black, in sharp contrast to the colourful daylight world of Lumberton. He is already dressed to descend into the town's dark underworld when he finds the severed ear.

Another classic wordless opening sequence occurs in *Apocalypse Now*. An establishing shot shows a jungle tree-line. US army helicopters appear and explosions set the jungle on fire as The Doors play on the soundtrack. We know instantly that we are witnessing a scene from the Vietnam War. Then we see the next scene superimposed over the burning jungle. First his eyes, then the haggard face of the central character, Willard, upside down, lying on a bed, smoking a cigarette. The helicopters he has been dreaming about turn into the whirring blades of the ceiling fan. Exploring his messy room, we see a half-drunk bottle of whisky and a gun by his pillow. Even before it is confirmed in Willard's voiceover, we know he is a dangerous man.

Close your eyes and see ...

- Think about your favourite films and recall any striking scenes which had a visual impact, particularly in terms of colour and image. Think about the way these images are used to tell a story. Do different colours have different significance? It is no accident that the red shoes in the fairytale eventually dance their wearer to death.

- Choose two colours. What images do they suggest? Maybe you think of blue and it suggests the sea, or the earth seen from space, and white, the colour of a space suit. Links will start to form – an astronaut returning from the moon to splash down in the Atlantic, perhaps.

- Using your colours and images as springboards, write a few opening scenes for an imaginary film. Forget about dialogue. Think about metaphorical images – helicopter blades and ceiling fan, twisted hose and sudden stroke. Introduce a character and their world. Try and create an atmosphere and a sense of antici-pation. Write in the present tense and only what you would see watching the action on screen.

THE PREMISE

The premise is a crystallisation of what your story is going to be about. Tell it in one or two sentences, or at most a few paragraphs. Outline its most significant aspects: *The Matrix* is about Neo, a computer programmer, who discovers he is living in a virtual world created by machines, learns he has the means to oppose them, and sets out to liberate humanity from their control.

What is the genre?

- Pick five films you have seen and write short premises for them. Whose story is it and what is the story about? Try not to be side-tracked by subplots. Many detective stories also contain a love story but the real premise is about the solving of the crime.
- Write several film premises of your own. Try different genres: a love story, a thriller, a comedy. Think in terms of a main character and the obstacles they must overcome. Give your character a name. Have fun. This is an exercise in using your imagination.

THREE-ACT STRUCTURE

Many screenwriters and industry professionals maintain that most commercial feature films follow a three-act structure. Although there is no curtain or commercial break, according to this notion feature films divide into three distinct parts: beginning, middle and end. While there are convincing arguments that no single all-embracing structure can be applied to all narrative construction, this approach does have its merits. Try using this model, if only to see if it works for you.

Act 1

The beginning takes up approximately the first 20 to 30 minutes of a 120-minute screenplay. The first act is the base on which the following acts build. It is where your story must be set up by introducing your main characters, the world they inhabit and the problem your protagonist must solve. An *inciting incident* – a dramatic event which upsets the balance of the protagonist's world, setting the main story in motion – usually occurs within the first ten minutes of Act 1.

Most of the exposition occurs during this act and everything that happens in the middle and end relates to elements it introduces. The first act should build to a crisis – a major setback or revelation for your protagonist.

Though you need to hook the audience with your fascinating characters and intriguing central problem as quickly as possible, be careful not to risk confusing the audience by introducing too many names and faces at once. Use established characters to introduce unknown characters. For example, in the first scene introduce Jack and Nicola. In the second scene Nicola leads us to her lover, Dave. In the third scene Jack goes for a drink with his two friends, Bob and Paul. In three scenes five characters have been introduced, but because we have met them gradually there is less chance of confusion than if all five appeared in Scene 1.

Tarantino is an example of a writer who understands conventions so well that he can play around with them, breaking up the chronological order of events in the three intersecting stories of *Pulp Fiction* and reordering them in a non-linear structure. But even in an ensemble film like this he is careful to introduce his multiple protagonists one or two at a time, and still manages to achieve a definite feeling of beginning, middle and end.

Act 2

The middle should be the longest act, roughly 70 minutes of a 120-minute script, where the narrative develops and new problems start to build. There should be a brief lull at the beginning of Act 2, after the climax of Act 1. Then you should slowly intensify the conflict and begin to develop subplots. A subplot is a secondary story strand which weaves in and out of your main story line. Your main story is your protagonist striving for a goal: a policewoman on the trail of a clever serial killer, for instance. A subplot may grow out of that conflict. The policewoman develops a relationship with an incarcerated psychopathic genius in order to get an insight which will help her catch the killer at large. Your subplot characters are usually introduced in Act 1 but their stories start to develop in Act 2.

You should start to develop new complications, building the conflict throughout Act 2. It should climax at a much higher pitch of dramatic tension than the crisis that ended Act 1.

Act 3

The end is the shortest act, taking up the final 20 minutes of a 120-minute script. Here you draw your story to a conclusion and provide a sense of closure. The audience should feel it is right that your story ends where it does. This act should begin with another brief respite, when the tension that ended Act 2 slackens off. But this is only the calm before the storm. The conflict should build quickly through a series of accelerating struggles to the climax. This is the point of maximum tension when your protagonist should either attain their goal or fail in the attempt.

After the climax, many films have a resolution scene, where plot ends are tied up, although a further question might be raised in the minds of the audience. The policewoman who has caught the serial killer may be at a congratulatory function when she receives a phone call from the now escaped psychopath, who sends his best wishes.

Looking at the three-act structure

- Watch films critically and see if they fit the dictates of three-act structure. Can you identify inciting incidents – and the climax points near the end of each act?
- Try breaking a story you know well into three component acts – beginning, middle and end – bearing in mind the separate functions of each act: to establish, develop and conclude.

KNOWING YOUR ENDING DICTATES YOUR BEGINNING

Before you start writing you need to know how your story ends. You do not need to know the entire story in detail, but the end dictates its beginning. If your hero is going to kill the villain with an unbelievable knife-throw at the end, it might be advisable to show that he used to be part of a circus knife-throwing act at the beginning. If you simply go ahead and write the script, it is possible that a knife-throwing ending may arrive without any of the prefiguring that will make it seem plausible.

It is like starting a journey. If you have a destination in mind, you do not necessarily have to take the most direct route. Though you detour to other places, your final destination will shape your journey. The end of your film shapes the elements you include in your script at the beginning. Robert Towne's screenplay for *Chinatown* concludes with the villain, Noah Cross, getting away with the murder of his son-in-law, the rape of his daughter and a massive fraud, while the private detective protagonist, Gittes, watches helplessly. This ending is foreshadowed in a line in the first scene where Gittes tells an enraged client, 'You've got to be rich to kill somebody, anybody, and get away with it.' Noah Cross is rich and he does get away with it.

> **The beginning of the end**
>
> ⊕   Look at the endings of several films, say the last ten minutes, on video or in script form. Then go back and look at the first ten minutes. See if you can spot the set-ups that are dictated by the closing scenes. You should see the themes of the films emerge.
>
> ⊕   Practise writing a couple of ending scenarios. Think about the way these endings would affect the beginning of your imaginary films.

CHARACTER

Protagonist

The majority of films have one central character. This is the protagonist, the person whose story is being told – someone with a problem to solve. He or she wants something, but obstacles are put in the way by someone or something antagonistic. Your story is about how the protagonist eventually overcomes the obstacles, or is overcome by them. Drama is about conflict and struggle.

In films with two or more protagonists, these central characters generally fall into one of two categories, what Robert McKee (1999) calls the plural-protagonist and the multi-protagonist. In films with plural-protagonists the story is driven by two or more characters with a shared desire or goal. Examples are *Thelma and Louise*, *The Seven Samurai* and *Calendar Girls*. In films with multi-protagonists, the characters follow separate goals, and these films tell multi-plot stories. Films like *Pulp Fiction* and *Magnolia* do this by interweaving several stories, each with its own central character.

Protagonists should have a powerful will which drives their need to achieve a goal. In *Blue Velvet*, Jeffrey's wilfulness drives the story. Finding the severed ear is the inciting incident which sets him on his investigative journey, but it is Jeffrey's headstrong nature that makes him continue to pursue this investigation against the advice of the police.

As well as being wilful and having a strong conscious desire, protagonists often have an unconscious desire that may act against what they are supposed to want. In Christopher Nolan's *Memento*, the protagonist struggles against his inability to make new memories as he tries to find his wife's murderer; but we eventually discover that continuing the quest for its own sake is all that gives his life meaning.

In a discussion with some students about the film *Witness*, there was disagreement as to whether the protagonist was John Book; the Amish boy, Samuel, who witnessed the murder; or his mother, Rachel. Although both Rachel and Samuel are introduced first, they prove to be the instruments that set John Book on the story's main physical and psychological journey. The murder is presented to the detective as a problem for him to solve. His dramatic need or desire is to bring the killer to justice. This is thwarted at the end of the first act when, despite discovering the murderer's identity, Book is forced to go on the run with the Amish mother and child. The man behind the murder is his own boss. In the second act, Book enters the strange world of the Amish. It is here that he experiences a different set of conflicts, those between his own feelings and values and those of the religious community, which leave him a changed man at the end of the film.

Your central character should be someone in perpetual physical or psychological motion, with the capacity to follow his or her desire to the end. Protagonists should also engage the audience's sympathy. This recognition of shared humanity will enable them to identify with the character and want them to achieve their goal. In *Chinatown*, Gittes follows a trail of clues to discover who has murdered Mulwray, stolen water, and set him up as a dupe. Although Gittes is self-regarding and opportunistic, his flaws are portrayed in a manner which engages the audience's sympathy. Ironically, it is one of these character flaws, Gittes' reckless egotism, which plays him into the hands of his antagonist, Noah Cross, and causes him to fail to save Evelyn Mulwray and her daughter.

Protagonists should change as a result of pressures exerted on them. Remember that drama is about conflict, which often occurs when two characters have mutually exclusive aims. In this sense, every protagonist needs to be opposed. This is the role of the antagonist.

Antagonist

The antagonist may be an individual or a combination of people whose purpose is to frustrate the protagonist's attempts to achieve his or her goal. The antagonist does not have to be a villain. It may not even be a person. It could be an evil scientist, an unscaleable mountain, a jealous ex-lover or an uncaring establishment. It may even be an aspect of the protagonist's own character, a fatal flaw which thwarts the character's attempts to achieve meaningful relationships. In Vincent Gallo's independent film *Buffalo 66*, the central character has to come to terms with his anger and misdirected need for revenge before he can accept the love of Christina Ricci's character and come to terms with the world.

Although you should always strive to create believable, well-rounded characters, you should be aware that they all serve a function, just as the protagonist's function is to pursue a goal. Many films include a character who functions as the protagonist's object of desire or 'love interest'. Also the central character often has a confidante – someone they trust and with whom they can drop their guard, showing vulnerability or other normally hidden aspects of their character. This role could be taken by a partner who may even be a second protagonist.

Catalyst

The important catalyst figure appears in almost every story, serving to push it forward and send the protagonist in new directions. The catalyst may be a witness to a crime who reports it to a detective, as Samuel does to John Book. It may be the British soldier who asks his IRA executioner to take a message to his girlfriend. They may only be minor figures and stories may have many catalysts.

Diverse characters

Films often have characters whose function is to provide comic relief, lightening the story by making the audience laugh, like the Rhys Ifans character in *Notting Hill*. Other characters may serve to highlight aspects of the protagonist's character through contrast. Thus a profligate protagonist may have a thrifty workmate, or a violent gangster may befriend a pious priest. Similarly, certain characters may be used to represent or express thematic concerns. In *Witness*, for instance, Eli represents the Amish non-violent way of life. You should, however, always strive to make these characters seem more than just functional. To do this, you need to get to know them thoroughly.

Character biographies

At the planning stage, make biographies of your major characters, describing how they look in an impressionistic way. Are they tall or short? Don't give their specific height or details such as hair or eye colour, unless these details are vital: you do not want to limit unnecessarily the choice of actors for the role. You do, however, need to give a sense of your characters' personalities.

Develop their back-stories. What were they doing before your story began? Most importantly, how did these events affect them emotionally? Ask them questions, and describe their general outlook. This will govern their response. What inner conflicts are the characters controlled by, or trying to control? How do they respond to each other? You may want to write several pages on each character. The more you know about them, the more credible they will become.

Edit these descriptions to just five or ten lines for major characters and three to five for minor ones. These condensed biographies may be used as part of a treatment package.

Closer to home

Write a one- or two-page biography of someone you know, then edit it to ten lines which convey their looks and personality traits.

PLANNING

Before writing your screenplay, you need to plan its overall structure through *scene cards, step outlines, treatments* and *outlines*. You should always write in the present tense. This is how your eventual screenplay will be written. The action is happening now. Avoid lapsing into the past tense.

Scene cards

Many writers put their basic scene ideas on index cards, using a separate card for each scene. In this way you can keep the story outline fluid and experiment with juxtapositions of key scenes to see how this affects the structure of the whole. Using the model of the three-act structure, you could begin with cards representing the inciting incident and each of your act climaxes and slowly add and subtract scenes as you build a step outline around them.

Step outline

A step outline tells the basic story in steps. It may be a list of key scenes, assembled from your scene cards, saying where each scene takes place, who is in it and briefly describing what happens. Though the step outline can be just a sequence of events, it could become a detailed scene-by-scene breakdown of the entire script, and end up closely resembling a screenplay without the dialogue. This sort of detailed outline will make your final scriptwriting task much easier.

Treatment

A treatment is a screenplay told in story form and is usually between two and 15 pages long. At this stage you have the freedom to write in a more literary style, which may help in establishing the mood of your film. It should flow in logical order from beginning to end and convey emotion as well as plot. Make clear why your characters behave as they do, what impact events have on them, and vice versa. The treatment should give the subtext – the thoughts and feelings behind what is said and done. You can indicate what people talk about, but without including the dialogue.

The treatment can serve two functions. First, it is a way of evaluating your story and characters before beginning the more detailed task of writing the script. You can see if your story makes sense and builds dramatically to its conclusion. By looking at the way one event relates to another you can see whether your story has direction or if it wanders off at a tangent.

Second, the treatment can function as a detailed selling document which tells the story in full to potential agents and/or producers. Some writers are offered development deals on the strength of treatments alone, before they have written a word of the actual script. Think of your treatment as the blueprint for your screenplay in the same way that your screenplay will be a blueprint for a film. You can always change things. As with your screenplay, nothing is set in stone.

The outline

The outline is a short treatment or synopsis which gives the premise and a plot outline, and mentions the main characters. It should be between one and four pages long and its main function is as a selling document to show to prospective agents and producers. Think of it as a review of a film not yet made. Outlines can be useful to gauge interest in a story idea before you turn it into a script, or to promote interest in an existing screenplay. Some people in the industry insist on outlines or treatments before they will look at full scripts. Others prefer to look at completed scripts, maintaining that an entertaining outline is no proof that an untried writer is capable of producing a good screenplay.

The outline

Write an outline of a film you have seen recently.

FORMAT FOR SCREENPLAYS

Screenplays should be word-processed in Courier 12-point and printed on a laser printer. Dialogue and visual directions should not be interrupted by page breaks. Write in simple, functional language, avoiding florid descriptions or overly literary phrases. Be specific and precise. Keep to the present tense. The action is always happening now, as it appears on screen.

Only production scripts contain camera angles and editing directions. These should not appear in submission scripts. The only directions of this type you should include are FADE IN at the top of the first page on the left-hand side and FADE OUT two spaces down on the left-hand side after the last line of your screenplay.

This is the format for a submission script. Its purpose is to present the basic story. The director and not the writer decides how that story is interpreted on the screen. The three necessary elements in a screenplay are:

* scene heading (interior or exterior, location, time)
* visual exposition (what you would see if you were watching the screen)
* dialogue.

The scene heading states where the following action and dialogue are taking place, and tells us the time of day. It says whether this is inside (INT) or outside (EXT). The geographical location comes next (LIVER-POOL), followed by the time (NIGHT). The scene heading is positioned on your first indent, ten spaces in from the left-hand side of the page. Here is an example:

EXT. LIVERPOOL CITY CENTRE. NIGHT

Every time the action moves to another location you must give another scene heading. Each room in a house, for instance, demands a separate scene. Remember that you can enter a scene at any point. You may, for instance, choose to show only the end of an argument.

The visual exposition describes the action taking place on the screen and should only contain what you would see as a viewer of the film. The characters' names should be capitalised the first time they appear in the script, but not subsequently. The first time a character appears, the name should be followed by a short physical description including age and build: for example, 20-ish, wiry, ugly. The visual exposition should be beneath the scene heading at the same indent position, ten spaces in from the left-hand side of the page. All lines should be single-spaced. For example:

MARNIE PEARSON, 30-ish, attractive, saunters into the room, looks around for a moment then flops into an armchair, staring at her husband, EDWARD, late 40s, wiry, who stands looking out the window. He turns and glares at her. Marnie gives him a defiant smile.

No explanation is given as to why Edward glares or Marnie smiles. The reasons for their behaviour will be revealed through their actions and dialogue. It is not necessary to include motivational explanations such as: Edward, angry at his wife's infidelity, looks mad. This will be revealed through dialogue.

DIALOGUE

Dialogue follows the visual exposition, with the character's name capitalised in the centre of the page. Their words follow on the next line, centred, with the left and right margins about 20 spaces in from each side of the page:

MARNIE
God! You're ugly when you frown.

Film dialogue is not real-life conversation. It should not meander, the way everyday conversation does, but should be economical and resonant. Lines should be short and spare. Try not to give one character more than three or four lines of dialogue at a time. If a character is giving a long speech, try and break it up either by interjections from other characters or by inserting bits of relevant visual exposition. This stops the script looking dialogue-heavy.

Make different characters speak with different rhythms, uses of language and sentence lengths. Their speech patterns and what they say should reveal things like cultural background, educational level and age. Your characters should speak for themselves rather than as conduits for information you want to give the audience. A certain amount of expository dialogue is inevitable, but it should be disguised or distracted from by having something else going on at the same time.

People do not always tell the truth and often say the opposite of what they mean. The subtext is what is going on behind the dialogue: the way a waiter may wish a customer 'Good evening, sir', while making an exasperated face at one of his colleagues. In film you can show a lot of non-verbal communication, so avoid stagy proclamations and, wherever possible, tell the story with action rather than words. Always remember, show don't tell.

Creating dialogue

⚬   Look at everyday situations, and the disparity between what people say and what they do. See how subtexts emerge out of conversations which appear to be about something else.

> Write a situation where two people talk while doing something everyday, like shopping or working. One of the characters wants to bring up something he or she feels is important. The other character keeps trying to steer the conversation in another direction. Give the two characters different speech patterns. See what you can reveal about them, as much by what they do not say as what they say.

WRITING FOR TELEVISION

While feature films are intended to be viewed by static audiences watching cinema screens, television programmes are geared to small-screen domestic viewing where the viewer may be doing other things while watching. Television narratives are interrupted by commercial breaks or broken into episodes. On one level, viewing is less concentrated than the cinema experience. On another, it can be more intimate and ongoing, as is reflected by the type of dramatic storytelling that seems best suited to the medium. Long-running series and soap operas with their repetitive and continually interweaving plots, with no resolution, dominate the schedules.

Television narratives are generally more dialogue-driven than those of the feature film. Their scale of events is usually smaller and their drama more domestic. Fewer characters can appear on the small screen in any one scene. The cinema's wide screen can show wonderful crowd scenes, but four is a crowd on television.

SHORT FILMS

These tend to be shown late at night on either BBC2 or Channel 4, and rarely get a cinema screening except at special festivals. There is currently, however, a renewed interest in short films. Primarily, they seem to function as show-reels for new directors, but they also offer writers a chance to demonstrate their skill. Channel 4's *Short and Curlies* season was specifically designed to encourage new writers.

The short short is usually under five minutes and tends to have the plant and pay-off structure of a joke. An example of this sort of narrative is Eric Christiansen's *I Mean It*, made for Film Four's *Shooting Gallery* season.

A husband watches his wife tie the front of her jogging shorts, telling her he suspects she is having an affair. She tells him not to be stupid and goes out for a run, during which she meets her lover in his van. As she pulls her clothes back on, the lover asks her if she has told her husband yet. She says she could not. She has realised she still loves him. The lover kicks her out of the van. Back home, she tells her husband they should go on a second honeymoon together. The husband goes to hug her but she says she needs a shower and turns to go to the bathroom. Suddenly the husband starts sobbing. While his wife wonders what is wrong, we see that the drawstring on her shorts is at the back.

ONE-OFF DRAMAS AND TWO-PART DRAMAS

Many older television writers and producers have bemoaned the demise of the single play. According to producer Tony Garnett, 'During one year in the middle of the sixties we put out thirty-four original full-length single dramas, each between 75 and 100 minutes long.' This was where a new generation of writers such as Dennis Potter and Ken Loach rose to prominence. One-off single dramas made for television have since been scarce. Jimmy McGovern's *Dockers* and *Sunday* are exceptions that spring to mind. More recently, the BBC has produced a series of single plays by different writers, updating *The Canterbury Tales*. ITV has produced the odd one-off drama like *Margery and Gladys*. It has also produced a slate of two-part dramas such as *Carla* and *Too Good to be True*. These tend to be overlong single dramas, cut in half and shown over two consecutive nights to maximise audience figures, and seem to be growing popular with television programmers.

SERIALS

Serial dramas consist of one story told over three to twelve instalments. They are usually written by a single writer and have the same overall creative continuity as a single drama or a feature film, but with a wider scope. Many serials are adapted from well-known novels, such as *Brideshead Revisited*, *Pride and Prejudice*, *The Thorn Birds* and *The Forsyte Saga*. Writers such as Paul Abbot, Lynda La Plante, Jimmy McGovern and the late Dennis Potter have produced original serial dramas like *State of Play*, *The Singing Detective*, *Prime Suspect* and *Cracker*. Stories like *Gormenghast* are ideally suited to the serial form. As its director Andy Wilson says, 'It doesn't have a movie structure ... It is a saga and with sagas you need space to expand.' Serial drama gives the audience time to live with the characters and can easily accommodate multi-protagonist stories.

DRAMA SERIES

Series are collaborative productions which use rotating teams of writers and directors but maintain a house style. Series feature the same core characters and settings in every self-contained episode. The audience becomes familiar with a group of characters, but can watch episodes in isolation without having to follow cliff-hanging plot lines.

However, series often incorporate serial elements into their storylines. This means that while a single episode of *Casualty* may tell a couple of self-contained stories, it will have other storylines involving the regular characters which continue throughout the series. These are known as serial story arcs, and are increasingly seen in more sophisticated series like *Six Feet Under*, where the continuing stories often provide the main interest. Even so, each episode always has at least one story that is concluded, usually concerning the funeral parlour's latest client.

Examples of long-running series which together with soap operas make up the bulk of television's dramatic programming are: *The Bill, Heartbeat, The Cops, Holby City, ER, 24, The West Wing, The Sopranos, Boomtown, Alias* and *Angel*.

SOAPS

Soaps are multi-protagonist serials which never end, mimicking real life. Their actors age with the characters they play. British soaps include *Coronation Street, EastEnders, Emmerdale* and *Hollyoaks*.

For many writers, soaps or drama series like *Casualty* and *The Bill* offer the most likely route to paid employment. Jimmy McGovern, writer of film and television dramas such as *Priest, Hillsborough, Cracker* and *Dockers*, began his professional writing career with *Brookside*. Frank Cottrell Boyce, writer of *Butterfly Kiss* and *Welcome To Sarajevo*, wrote for *Coronation Street*. Tony Jordan, creator of the police series *City Central*, was given his first break on *EastEnders*.

Generally, soaps have regular storylining sessions in which future events are worked out and broken down into episode storylines. These storylines are given to individual writers who then write the episode, bearing in mind continuity. While most soaps have their writers attend regular storylining sessions, others have separate storyliners who provide their writers with detailed scene-by-scene breakdowns for which they provide dialogue rather than plot.

Writers' creative freedom varies from soap to soap and probably with the status of the writer. Soaps, like long-running series, have an ever-evolving document called a bible which writers can refer to. This contains a list of episodes to date, what has been covered in them and biographies of the characters. If the series revolves around a specialised area like the police force or the medical profession, the bible will include details of procedure and organisational structure.

Potential writers may be asked to submit a sample of their work. Then they may be offered the opportunity to write a trial script. This can take different forms. *Hollyoaks* asks writers to produce half an episode with a limited number of characters and locations on a theme the script editor or producer suggests. They will expect you to display familiarity with the characters and their current storyline and you will be given a limited time to produce it. *Family Affairs* gives rookie writers a copy of a full episode outline to translate into scenes and dialogue.

SITCOMS

Situation comedies are generally 30 minutes long and, in common with drama series, feature a small core of characters in each self-contained episode. Within these characters there is usually either one whose story dominates, determining the course of action – for example, David Brent in *The Office* and Basil in *Fawlty Towers* – or there is a conflicting relationship which dominates the action, like that of Niles and Frasier in *Frasier*. Sitcoms usually take place in one or two central locations. If the show becomes very successful, the number of locations may grow. The writer's aim is to generate humour from the characters' attempts to confront their problems and deal with each other. With a few exceptions such as *Mr Bean*, this is mainly done through dialogue. Examples of situation comedy are: *Phoenix Nights, The Royle Family, Father Ted, The League of Gentlemen, Only Fools and Horses, Friends, Will and Grace* and *Seinfeld*.

CONCLUSION

Writing for film and television is a collaborative art, so from the outset you will need to cultivate a willingness to revise and redraft your work, and to see your script as only part of a process, not a completed product. Screenwriting may enable you to reach a wider audience than any other medium, but the competition is fierce. Perhaps more than any other kind of writer, the person who submits their work to a production company or television channel needs to be professional, determined and immune to discouragement.

Do not be afraid of involving yourself in the production side: it can only enhance your understanding of the writing process. Identify local companies and producers whose work you admire and send them your script. Cultivate any contacts you make. Today's producer on local television may be tomorrow's Tarantino.

8 WRITING FOR STAGE

Dymphna Callery

'for the author and then for the actor the word is a small visible portion of a gigantic unseen formation'.

Peter Brook

INTRODUCTION

The stage is a medium of the imagination, conjuring images in the spectators' minds. At the opening of Shakespeare's *Henry V*, the Chorus asks 'can this cockpit can hold / The vasty fields of France?', inviting us to imagine whole battalions of soldiers when we see just one. Language and illusion provoke the spectators' imaginations into seeing what is not there, but what action and words suggest is there. The power of theatre resides in suggestion rather than the imitation of reality. As Peter Brook (1968) says, 'the best production takes place in the mind of the beholder'.

The vehicle for drama is not print but flesh and blood: living breathing actors, moving, still, speaking, silent, in front of our eyes in the present moment. Theatre is a live event, an experience shared between audience and actors.

GETTING STARTED

No one is going to curl up in bed with your play. You are writing for live performance. Playscripts are templates for performance rather than blueprints. Actors, directors and designers bring their particular skills and ideas to interpreting a text, for theatre is a collaborative art. Acknowledging the unique properties of theatre will enable you to exploit its potential and avoid the beginner's problem of writing 'talking heads' where people sit on sofas and explain themselves rather than move around and 'act'. There is little point in writing an unperformable play.

Create a 'theatre of the mind' where you can watch events unfold. It will help if you see as wide a range of work as you can, as it will enhance your awareness of what is possible. Go and sit in an empty theatre and soak up the atmosphere. Try sitting in different places. Ask if you can stand on the stage. This will give you some sense of the nature of the space itself. Try speaking. Imagine the theatre full, the spectators watching your play.

ACTION

Molière declared that all he needed was a couple of planks and a passion or two. At its simplest the stage is an empty space where anything can happen, and the word 'drama' means action. Imagine an empty stage. Someone enters and finds a letter. They open the letter, read it and tear it into little pieces. They leave. Nothing has been said, yet anyone watching is intrigued. See this happening in your mind's eye. What is in the letter? Who is the person reading it? Decide. Now work out what happens next.

Three different suggestions might be:

- The same person returns and picks up the scraps of paper bar one, and leaves.
- Another person enters and picks up the scraps and tries to jigsaw them together.
- A clown throws the scraps of paper up in the air and pretends it is snowing.

Follow any of these, or your own suggestion, with two further scenes. See how far you can get without using any dialogue, discovering the characters' responses to situations in physical terms: that is, what they *do* rather than worrying about what they say.

David Mamet (1994) likens drama to fairytales, because characters and situations are presented straightforwardly in terms of what happens. 'The essential task of drama', he says, 'is to induce us to suspend our rational judgment, and to follow the *internal* logic of the piece.' So, for example, we suspend our rational judgment with Goldilocks or Cinderella, merely following the order of events – the story.

> **Write a scenario**
>
> Consider what you have written. Try to work out a logical sequence of events, however surreal. To develop the piece, you may introduce a maximum of three performers, and other objects if you wish, provided that people interact with them, but avoid furniture unless you use it in a playful manner (chairs turning into a car, a bed becoming a mountain, for example). Write only the bare essentials, and do not describe anything or anyone – simply what happens. Write up to five 'scenes'. This is called a 'scenario' which can be developed further by adding dialogue and creating more events from the situations therein.

It is important to recognise that spectators 'read' visual signals. Every action and gesture on stage is a 'sign', and objects, costume, lighting effects all relay information which spectators will interpret, just as you decided what happened with the letter. Nothing should be on stage without a reason for being there; everything on stage *serves* the action. This applies to words too.

DIALOGUE

Dialogue has three principal functions:

* to embody action
* to move the story on
* to reveal/conceal character.

It is useful to think, as Mamet does, of speech as 'verbal behaviour' which does more than just convey information. Using simple dialogue exercises as starting points can generate ideas for characters and situations. Think of dialogue as there to intrigue rather than inform. Human beings often reveal more by what they do not say than what they do say, and imply rather than state what they mean.

> **Yes: yes**
>
> Write a scene between two people, A and B, where the only word used is 'Yes' and its variations, e.g. 'Yeah', 'Okay', 'Uh-huh'. Use punctuation, pauses and silence; you may repeat a word within the same line. A maximum of ten exchanges will do. Ideally, enlist others to read out the results. They will inflect the lines according to both the punctuation and how their partner inflects their lines. You may be surprised that these are not what you had in mind, and that a situation and relationship emerges beneath the 'conversation', perhaps even some sense of character.

However life-like, dramatic dialogue is not a replica of normal conversation; it is the arrangement of words in an authentically rhythmical pattern which imitates the cadences of everyday speech. This arrangement is designed for maximum dramatic impact, and is essentially a writer's conjuring trick.

Record and condense

Choose a public place, such as a café or a train carriage, where you can listen to people talking. Keeping your notebook discreet, write down the dialogue between two strangers you overhear. Try to record *exactly* what they say, including gaps, repetitions and expletives. At home, read this out and try to work out (a) what their relationship is and (b) what they are talking about. Bearing in mind the previous 'Yes' exercise, write ten lines of *dramatic* dialogue based on this.

The full conversation has to be condensed, but retain clues as to situation and character. A playwright works like a translator, invariably saying far less than the original speaker. Try varying and limiting the number of words in any line, say to a maximum of ten, and see what effect that has.

Four paragraphs ago you were invited to write what happens without using speech. Now transpose the action of those scenes into dialogue, using speech as a gloss on what happens. Try to avoid the characters describing the action. So rather than:

A   (*Tears letter*) I'm going to tear this letter.

You might have:

A   (*Tears letter*) No!

What your characters say will depend on the scenario that emerged from your 'letter' scenes and the action that arose. Yet the more 'indirect' the dialogue, the more you intrigue your audience.

STORY AND PLOT

You do not necessarily start with a whole story. You may start with an idea about characters, situation, fragments of story or even a few lines of dialogue, and develop your play from those. But by practising with a story you know, you can extend your understanding of the process of playwriting.

Let us take the story of Goldilocks and the Three Bears and, bearing in mind the previous exercises, write the action and dialogue:

Scene 1
Three Bears *sit down to breakfast. The porridge is steaming.*
Small Bear   Ow!
Medium Bear   He's burnt his mouth.
Big Bear   We'll go for a walk till it's cool.
They go.

Scene 2
Goldilocks *enters. She tastes the porridge in each bowl, finally eating all in the small bowl.*
Goldilocks   Too hot! Yuk. Too sweet. Cor! Yum. Yum.
She tries each chair and settles on the smallest one. It breaks.
Goldilocks   Ow!
She yawns.
She tests each bed and lies on the smallest one. She falls asleep.

Scene 3
The **Three Bears** *enter.*
Big Bear   Someone's been eating my porridge!
Medium Bear   Someone's been eating my porridge!
Small Bear   Mine's all gone!
Big Bear   Someone's been sitting in my chair!
Medium Bear   Someone's been sitting in my chair!
Small Bear   Mine's all broken.
Big Bear   Someone's been lying on my bed.
Medium Bear   Someone's been lying on my bed.
Small Bear   Look!
Goldilocks *wakes.*
Goldilocks   Aaaahhh!
Big Bear   Grab her!
Medium Bear   Missed!
Small Bear   Come back. Come back!
They chase her from the house.

The story is embodied in the actions, reactions and interactions of the characters in that situation. Story is essentially *character* plus *situation*.

Consider the plot as an obstacle course designed to make a character's journey more engaging and even difficult. The twists and turns of the plot arise from making it hard for your characters to get what they want. Macbeth, for example, decides he wants to be king. Duncan is his first obstacle. What if he kills him? Having removed him, King Macbeth sees Banquo as the obstacle to being 'safely thus', again asks 'What if ...?' and then removes him. Every time he removes an obstacle another one takes its place.

Dramatise a fairy story

Take a simple fairy story and dramatise it as we did with Goldilocks. Add substance to it by asking questions and letting your imagination supply possible answers. Try modernising the story by asking questions with a contemporary ring, such as: What if Goldilocks searches for salt and finds a cache of drugs? Supposing the porridge is spiked? These will lead you on, allowing a topical story to develop organically whilst still preserving the functions of the characters and the situation.

What you are seeking is *conflict*, the linchpin of a good plot.

It is dangerous to view conflict as merely loggerhead argument. That way lie the dreaded talking heads. Conflict can exist between character and authority, character and society, character and institution. Conflict arises out of the dilemmas characters face. The obvious example here is *Hamlet*, where the whole play grows from the protagonist's internal conflict as to whether or not to avenge his father.

THEME

The story of a play might be what happens on the surface but it is not what your play is really about. This is where the stage play often differs from the screenplay, which tends to be driven by narrative. *Waiting for Godot*, for example, is not simply a story of two tramps waiting for someone who never appears. Its theme is existential angst. In *Macbeth*, Shakespeare probes the source and impact of ambition. In *The Cherry Orchard*, Chekhov presents variations on the theme of unrequited love.

When drama deals with the struggles of individuals caught up in big events, it focuses on the universal human subject. Brecht places Mother Courage and her cart against the backdrop of the Thirty Years War: the history of that particular conflict is not as important as the way war reduces human relationships to the fiscal. The theme, in this case, shapes and sustains the momentum of the story.

To some extent a play is a 'working through' of a problem, often grounded in social or ethical concerns. The idea of using drama to proselytise has been around for centuries. The church used dramatic reconstructions of biblical stories to reach an illiterate audience in the Middle Ages. The Suffragettes mounted plays which espoused their cause to attract audiences to their meetings. Post-war British theatre abounds with cleverly argued dramas promoting socialism, feminism, anti-racism, gay rights, sympathy for the plight of HIV-positive victims. All these testify to drama's potential as polemic. In such plays characters represent specific attitudes towards an issue; the resulting conflict is usually resolved in a way that encourages the audience to side with the underdog.

When characters represent political positions they tend towards stereotype or caricature, depending on the degree of satirisation. Pillorying attitudes you do not agree with can be great fun, and there is therapeutic delight in controlling characters who represent attitudes you deplore and ensuring they get their comeuppance. Act 1 of Caryl Churchill's *Cloud Nine*, for example, presents a highly effective satire of Victorian imperialism and patriarchal ideology. But what distinguishes this play from other issue plays is the way Churchill exploits the imaginative possibilities of theatre: when the Victorian characters reappear in Act 2, set in the 1970s, they have aged only 25 years, and attempt to work out the dysfunctional relationships they have inherited from the past. Although the first act presents an array of stereotypes, the second act reinvents them as unique individuals with contradictions, struggling to make sense of their world.

When you read plays, always try to work out what the theme is and sum it up as simply as possible: for example 'love vs duty', or 'blood is thicker than water'. As you develop your play, identify what theme you are exploring and keep it in mind.

What if ...?

Take a simple newspaper item – tabloids are useful for this – and dramatise it by writing the action and dialogue. Expand the plot by asking 'What if ...?' and following up the ideas in terms of the theme. Ask what *attitudes* the characters represent in relation to the theme. In other words what matters to them? This is where you start asking questions of them in order to move the piece beyond a scenario.

CHARACTER

Characters are revealed by how they respond to situations and events through *action*, *reaction* and *interaction*. Speech is a component, but is the tip of an iceberg. The real business goes on beneath the surface. And an audience wants to work out why characters do what they do. Leaving room for them to guess keeps them involved.

If you already know everything about your characters your play will be lifeless. The trick is to let them tell you what is happening, to let them reveal themselves gradually. As Paul Mills (1996) says, you research your characters while you are writing them. The 'Yes, yes' exercise earlier gave you some idea of how characters emerge through the process of writing simple dialogue. Deciding your characters' *attitudes* in relation to a chosen theme enables you to provoke conflict and tension.

Attitude

Assign A and B oppositional attitudes towards a chosen theme. Start with a few lines of dialogue between them, using only variants of simple words like 'Yes' with punctuation and pauses as before, but keep their attitudes uppermost in your mind. Now let the dialogue continue using words for a few exchanges. Try to incorporate the advice in the section on dialogue so that you keep it focused.

In the following example, the theme is 'love vs duty' and the characters are siblings caught in the dilemma of who is to care for their father. The resulting dialogue might run:

A	Yes?
B	Okay.
A	You agree?
B	I said okay.
A	Meaning?
B	I'll do my share.
A	Do you love him?
B	Of course.
A	It's not a question of having to.
B	He's my father.

Gradually you start to get an idea of what each character's position is and what they want.

Like action and words, characters must serve the play. You need to allow them time to develop, to ferment. 'Writing a play is a quest', says Sheila Yeger (1990), and in the early stages you are finding out who the characters are and what your play is about.

Remember also that in art as in life human beings are flawed, vulnerable and deceitful, even when they are heroic! Humans are full of contradictions, which is what makes them unique and interesting. And if you give the best lines to the villain, your play will be the richer.

Although you want to create characters with individual traits, it is more important to ask questions of them than accumulate details. An actor cannot play shoe-size. Hot-seating is a game that encourages you to discover more about your characters.

The hot-seat

Let each playwright take a turn in the 'hot-seat' and the others fire questions at them, such as 'What do you vote?', 'What's your favourite book/TV programme/film?' and the 'hot-seater' replies on behalf of one of the characters in their play. Avoid questions about personal habits and physical appearance, and focus instead on attitudes. You need to know what *matters* to your characters. Ask and respond quickly – one minute per playwright.

You may be surprised by your answers! But such spontaneity can offer a direct line to a character's impulses. In real life we act and speak spontaneously. To be credible, characters must appear to do so.

SPEECHES

Writing monologues for your characters is an excellent way of getting inside them. A monologue offloads what is on their mind. They may comment on the action, offer their opinion, state their case, or even explode into an aria of expression. Lucky's long speech in the middle of *Waiting for Godot* is an extraordinary outburst which encapsulates the despair of language ever holding meaning.

You are allowing your characters to share their thoughts in a 'private' or 'public' manner, depending on the style of play. The former is a kind of internal monologue to which an audience is privy, and the character may or may not acknowledge them. The latter is where characters acknowledge the presence of the audience openly, more in the manner of 'stand-up', and is more common in issue plays. Read Chapter 9, 'Writing for radio', for a step-by-step guide on how to write a monologue.

What characters want is termed *motivation*. This includes their drives and their conscious and unconscious desires, so each character will have their own agenda. This emerges when they are put under pressure, as in the following exercise:

Character-speak

Take one of the characters you have been working with in any exercise so far. Pinpoint a moment where they are under pressure, and write a speech expressing what they feel. Experiment with private and public versions. What have you discovered about them?

SUBTEXT

Characters will pursue their desires by devious means, intentionally and unintentionally. And an audience wants 'to find out who wants what from whom' (Mills, 1996). This is where motivation links with subtext. At its simplest, subtext is what characters feel/think/want but do not say. The art of playwriting is to some extent the mastery of subtext: setting up conflicting desires without stating them.

What they want

Write a scene between your two characters where one gets what they want without stating it. Make it clear where they are and what is desired. Use any of the characters and situations which have emerged in the exercises so far.

Following on from the scene above, Alice is preparing to bury the now-dead father in the garden and wants her brother Bob's help:

Alice *digs.* **Bob** *watches.*
Bob   We can't bury him here. It's illegal.
Alice   When did he ever care about legality?
Bob   You'll get caught.
Alice   Not if you don't tell.
Pause.
Bob   This is a garden. It's not consecrated ground.
Alice   He was an atheist. *Pause.* I'm only doing what he wanted, Bob.
Bob   Where's the other shovel?

Notice how the power shifts between the characters as though, as in a tennis match, the exchanges become a rally with points being scored.

All human interaction functions in terms of status. It is the see-saw principle upon which the power shifts in relationships. Assigning status is a useful way of differentiating your characters and 'the gap between assumed and assigned status is a rich source of conflict' (Yeger, 1990). A classic status relationship is that of master/servant. A more subtle illustration of a relationship founded on mutual dependence can be found between Vladimir and Estragon in *Waiting for Godot* .

You can observe status by watching your friends and assigning them status numbers: 1 = someone who plays low, 10 = someone who plays high, with degrees in between. Once you have grasped the principle, try assigning your characters status numbers. You can play with status by either maintaining their number, or by getting low to 'play' high and vice versa. Comedy often operates on this principle; for example, a servant playing high status when the master is not looking.

Changing status

Consider your own version of the subtext exercise. Who has the higher status at the beginning? And who is higher at the end of the scene? Experiment with exaggerating the status shifts either by speech or action in a new draft. The aim is to 'up the stakes' at each point.

A modified version of the previous scene might run:

Alice *digs furiously.* **Bob** *watches.*
Bob   You can't bury him here. It's illegal.
Alice   Illegal ! Since when did you care about legality?
Bob   You'll go to prison.
Alice   Only if you tell.
Bob *kicks the ground.*
Bob   This is an allotment for godsake. It's not even consecrated ground.
Alice   He was an atheist. *(She rests on her spade)* I'm only doing what he wanted, Bob.
Bob   All right then. Where's the other shovel?

The amendments are slight but the see-saw is more obvious. It does not necessarily make a better script, but it reveals more about the undercurrents of this relationship. The scene is also moving closer to comedy, partly because the choice of 'allotment' rather than 'garden' is more absurd, partly because the characters seem more like bickering siblings.

Notice how the plot is beginning to develop. We have two major scenes, one before the father's death from an earlier exercise, and one after. Asking 'What if someone finds out?' can provoke a final outcome: for example, Alice is prosecuted for breaking the law, and Bob commits perjury by stating he knew nothing of the illegal burial.

STRUCTURING THE WHOLE

Now you have several short scenes and a monologue. If these are connected thematically you might have the beginnings of a play, especially if you have an ending in mind. Endings are like punchlines, both inevitable and surprising. They also present a kind of summing up of the play. At the end of *Hamlet* and *Macbeth*, carnage is accompanied by insight. Beckett's two tramps talk of going but stay. Brecht's Mother

Courage still pulls her cart across Europe. Alice and Bob replay sibling rivalry in public. Knowing the ending means that you can work towards it.

Mapping

Take a group of scenes from any of the previous exercises, either an adaptation of a fairytale or the 'letter' exercise or the newspaper item, and decide on an ending for the story. Now work out what needs to happen to lead to that point. Do not write any more just yet. At this point you are merely creating the map of what happens before deciding how to organise the journey of the play.

Reading plays is helpful. You discover how playwrights organise their material to create dramatic effects. Sometimes plays are organised in a manner which allows several stories to be connected by theme, rather than fitting into one overarching narrative like Hollywood movies. Some of the most vibrant modern plays utilise non-linear structures where the onus on interpreting narrative(s) and meaning(s) lies with the spectator. Yet the best plays still offer an audience a coherent experience. *Waiting for Godot* has a perfectly balanced two-part structure which works like counterpoint and suits the tragicomic nature of the play. Charlotte Keatley's *My Mother Said I Never Should* combines naturalistic scenes of four generations of women with surreal scenes between the characters as children. The dream-like structuring brings it closer to the landscape of memory than the map of history without losing a sense of mounting tension, climax and resolution normally ascribed to classic narrative structure.

It is how you assemble the elements of your play that gives it coherence. You may choose to make your theme clear by juxtaposition and contrast, or follow the story of a protagonist, or present a collage-poem in the manner of Ntozake Shange's *For Colored Girls Who Have Considered Suicide When The Rainbow Is Enuf*. Whatever your choice of structure, the purpose is to take your audience on a journey, and here the Aristotelian elements of conflict, mounting tension and resolution (or at least restoring order to chaos) provide a valuable model.

Having decided what kind of structure you are using, you need to break down the journey of the play into sections. Plays are made up of scenes, each one a unit which either introduces a new idea or develops those of previous scenes in a new location or different time. Each scene moves us on to another episode, yet each one operates like a mini-play, embodying conflict, tension and moving *towards* a resolution, which may be the source of further conflict.

Divide and rule

Go back to the previous exercise, and divide the 'map' you have devised into scenes. It is a good idea to give them titles as well as numbers, so, for example, 'Alice appears in court' might be the title of the next part of our illegal burial story.

Every scene needs a purpose or *objective* in relation to the whole. Once your theme and characters start to emerge and you have a map of the whole play in your head, you can assign objectives to each scene. This is where everything starts to coalesce and you know what each character wants *in each scene* and what part of the story happens *in each scene*. It is like putting a jigsaw together with pieces of varying size and shape. Remember that varying the length of scenes will create a more interesting rhythmic pattern for the whole.

Assign objectives to each scene, then write them with those objectives in mind. Start them as late as possible, as though you are moving in on people deep in conversation, and leave before they have finished.

Bear in mind that there needs to be some degree of urgency. 'Putting a clock on a scene' is an excellent method for injecting tension. Take one of the scenes you have written and revise it on the basis that either (a) someone else is due to arrive, or (b) one character has another pressing engagement. Try to avoid phrases like 'I have to go', or 'so-and-so is coming'.

Now you are beginning to write the first draft of a play. This will necessarily go through several drafts and be edited and redrafted if it gets into rehearsal. Asking drama students to read out your script will also teach you what 'works', whether a line 'rings true' or not, where the rhythm is awkward, when boredom sets in. Inevitably you will get it wrong! That is how you learn.

CONCLUSION

The best way to learn is to observe how other dramatists do it. Watching and reading plays extends your knowledge of the medium, and the plays referred to in this chapter are suggestions for reading. Better still, if you have an opportunity to watch rehearsals or drama workshops, or attend a local youth theatre or student drama group, then take it. Gaining experience of what happens in the theatre-making process will provide insights you can exploit. Playwriting is a process of trial and error, but ultimately the action and words need to work in that extraordinary three-dimensional empty space we call the theatre.

9 WRITING FOR RADIO

Aileen La Tourette

'The voice is a second face.'
Gerald Bower

INTRODUCTION

Radio is a wonderful medium for a writer. There are no restrictions on your imagination. You can move time around at will, create separate worlds, play whatever tricks you like to get your meaning across. The dead can speak, the inanimate come to life. All you need do is cue your listeners so they can imagine with you. You are issuing them with an invitation to come with you into another world, familiar or unfamiliar, contemporary or historical, realistic or surreal. It can be whatever you want it to be, provided you can bring it to life inside the listeners' heads. Radio is imagination speaking to imagination.

On a practical level, it is far cheaper to 'stage' a radio drama than to shoot a film, or mount a theatre production. Your work has more chance of being heard than it has of being seen, especially if you explore some of the possibilities discussed at the end of the chapter.

BEGINNING

If you want to write for radio – to write drama, perhaps, or adapt a classic book – the first thing you have to do is listen. Sound is what radio is about, even more than words.

Listen up

- If you live in a city, listen to its sounds with your eyes closed. What do you hear from the top of a bus, in the underground, on the street? If you live in the country, what do you hear, and when?
- Try listening at different times of the day and night. How do the noises change?
- Now try the exercise in different spaces. What sounds create the atmosphere of an office, classroom, library, church? Are there different 'sounds of silence'? If so, how?

Learning the medium

- Develop the habit of listening to radio. Turn it on at odd moments and get a feel for which programmes are broadcast when, how long they last, and who they are aimed at.
- Listen to radio drama, to the classic serial.
- Read radio previews and reviews. Buy the *Radio Times* and see how plays are described. Which descriptions make you want to listen?

STARTING YOUR PLAY

Writing a monologue is a good way to begin. Only one person is speaking: to another person, other people, or themselves. A monologue may be spoken by an inner voice. It may include other voices, echoes from the character's memory, or fantasies in which they imagine their future. Think of Alan Bennett's *Talking Heads*, a series of monologues that worked brilliantly on TV, and were equally effective on radio, with writer and listener engaged in a creative collaboration.

A character in a monologue talks freely, and may reveal things usually kept secret. You may have somebody watering plants, or wheeling a baby in a pram and telling it things that cannot be revealed to anyone who would really understand. Remember to contextualise your monologue. In other words, you need to find a device, such as the baby in the pram, to make it plausible that your character would be talking to themselves.

You may object that *Talking Heads* are not contextualised; and neither are Spalding Grey's monologues, another useful example. They simply begin, providing their own context. But Bennett and Grey are giants of the genre, and we are talking about a monologue that might be embedded in a play. You need to show that you know the rules before you can break them. Still, all rules are made to be broken; including that one.

The morning after

- Does a room sound different when there has been an argument in it? Or a party? How would a character in a radio play express the feeling of a 'morning-after' party room or bedroom?
- Imagine the words he or she would use, the sounds they might make clearing up, or making the bed. Imagine what might be going on in their mind.
- Now write a brief morning-after speech for such a character. They might speak their monologue aloud, or in the echoey tone that tells you the character is thinking the speech, saying it inside their own head. This is indicated in a script by the words *To us,* or *V.O.* for *voiceover.*
- Try your morning-after monologue both as voiceover and as a speech delivered aloud. Have someone read it, at first without any direction from you. Can they make sense of it? If not, you may have left too much of it inside your own head and not delivered it onto the page. You know what you are trying to say. Your actor does not, unless you tell them clearly. Do not assume that any lack of understanding is their fault. It may be yours.
- When you think the monologue is right, have them read it again.
- Describe the character to them, and then direct them, telling them how to get your intended emphasis. When you are satisfied, record their performance, noting how long it is – that is, how much time it takes, not how many pages. You may be surprised how short your work is, once it is spoken. You should get into the habit of timing every radio piece you write.

CHARACTER AND MOTIVE

Have a look back at Chapter 1 to remind yourself of the uses of your writer's notebook. Pick characters from supermarket queues, from trains and buses. What about the man or woman behind the checkout counter, or the bus driver, or the ticket collector? How long have they been doing their job? Try to avoid clichés. They might be thrilled to be working, escaping from tedium and poverty. They might be reaching for independence. Do not make assumptions, make observations. Imagine hearing the noises – the bleeps of the scanner, train rhythms, the bus engine – all day long. Maybe they are saving up for something. What?

You can repeat this exercise in any setting – waiting rooms, lecture rooms. Establish the background noises which deliver the atmosphere, so that the listener will know where they are (unless you want to keep them in suspense!). You cannot entirely separate character and setting, especially in a play. People behave in certain ways in particular places and situations. At the dentist's, for instance, some people react nervously, others show bravado. Ask someone to listen with you, and see what they get from your work. There may be unexpected dips, and also places where it takes off unexpectedly.

Now imagine what might have come before the scene in which the monologue is set, and what after. Improvise these scenes with your actor. Your characters will speak to each other, in real time, in memory, in fantasy – however you like. In a one-person show, one character will 'do' all the voices. But there will still be voices – in the plural.

The morning after, part 2

* Imagine that another character has overheard the monologue you wrote for the previous exercise, if your character has spoken aloud. If not, imagine the second character has been watching them. Will this character reveal their presence, or not? You must know why or why not, which means understanding motivation.
* You now have the workings of a plot. If they do reveal themselves, how will the first character react? Why? You may use dialogue (see below).

DIALOGUE

Think about dialogue in the widest sense, involving sound as well as words. There is a dialogue of wood and saw, a dialogue of vegetable board and chopper. How a character saws, or chops, will tell you about their mood. It might be more effective to begin a scene with a furious or frantic chopping of vegetables than with someone saying how angry or nervous they are about preparing dinner for their family or lover. Or you could begin with a slammed door. Is someone leaving, or is a storm brewing? Any sound effect which sets up questions in the listeners' minds makes a good start. Music is another form of dialogue which works well on radio, and can be highly useful in establishing mood.

People in plays – or books, for that matter – do not speak like people in real life. Their dialogue is more allusive, more subtle. You need to prune the boringness and repetition in order for speech to work in a play, unless you are using these attributes – boringness and repetitiveness – as a feature, perhaps for humour. Even if you are, your dialogue will be structured. Learn to glean the essence of a conversation and deliver it in tight, condensed form. This is what developing an ear for dialogue really means.

> **Greetings and farewells**
>
> * Improvise this exercise with friends, or perhaps with a local drama group. Act out as many hellos and goodbyes as you can imagine. You may be frostily polite or warmly passionate. You may be greeting your partner or long-lost parent – from the deck of a ship or the threshold of a room.
> * See what dialogue emerges. Keep it brief. Never pad unless this is what your characters are doing, to cover up a tense moment.

INDIRECT DIALOGUE

Develop an ear for what remains unspoken. Your dialogue will need to suggest what characters feel, as well as carry meanings they might not intend, or be trying to avoid. This is *indirect dialogue*, defined by Martin Esslin (1991) as 'the characters' oblique reference to the subject under discussion, since they cannot find the courage to express their feelings openly'. Esslin also notes that 'Chekhov used indirect dialogue in situations when the characters are too shy to express their real thoughts and hide their emotions behind trivial subjects'. Think of people talking about the weather. Are they sometimes talking about something else, to do with the way they feel? If it is sunny and someone shivers and says, yes, but it is too cold, could they not be talking about their inner state as well as the outer one? People find ingenious ways of talking about things, or not talking about them.

Suppose a mother is waiting at home for her son. She has had a phone call from the school, informing her that he has not turned up for the past two weeks. He comes in at the usual time:

> *Heavy rain, and thunder. Outer door slams. Sound of someone running upstairs.*
> **Gerry:**   [*shouts*] Mum?
> **Mum:**   I'm in the kitchen. [*To us*] Why does he always shout?
> *Gerry comes in.*
> **Mum:**   You're dripping! I just washed that floor.
> **Gerry:**   Cleaner now, innit? Any biscuits about?
> **Mum:**   You know where. Did you walk home alone?
> **Gerry:**   Yeah. No. With Paul.
> **Mum:**   Paul who?
> **Gerry:**   You know. Paul.
> **Mum:**   The older boy.
> **Gerry:**   [*mouth full of biscuit*] Bit oldern me. Yeah.
> **Mum:**   Likes to walk in the rain, does he?

Gerry: Ain't got a lot of choice today.
Mum: Choice. Now there's an interesting word.
Gerry: What's up with you, mum? You stuck inside all day or some-think?
F/X Baby starts to cry
Mum: As you said, son, I don't have a lot of choice.
F/X Mum sweeps out of the room
Gerry: [*To us*] Hate it when she calls me son. She sounds like she knows - no, she couldn't. [*Shouts*] Mum, what are we having for tea?

Note the use of *to us* to indicate that Gerry is speaking inside his head. Note also the spacing and script layout. Stage directions – using words like *Shouts* – should be kept to the minimum. *F/X* indicates sound effects. Here is another example of indirect dialogue:

F/X Sound of someone chopping vegetables, very fast and loud. Prison kitchen background of radio playing sad popular song, whistling, bit of banter, bubbling pots. Sound of keys on a chain as an officer unlocks the door, comes in, locks it.

Officer: Not blubbing, are we? Big lad like you?
Albert: Chopping onions, aren't I?
Officer: Ah. Onions.
Albert: Want to chop some, Mr. Allen?
Officer: Uh no thanks, Al. You go right ahead and cry, son [*laughs and moves away, whistling*].
Albert: [*softly*] Tosser.
F/X Chopping stops
Albert: [*To us*] Bet you could chop onions and not shed a tear. Bet you don't know how to cry. Bet you forgot. Mr Ex-army. I intend to see that onions are on the menu every day I'm in this kitchen, Mr Allen. Onions, onions and more onions [*crying hard now*]. That way I might just stay human. In spite of you. In spite of this place. In spite of these bloody, bloody onions.
F/X Chopping resumes

Give your characters individual voices. The listener needs to know who is speaking at all times, without confusion. The dialogue must contain tension which builds towards a release or revelation. The release may come or not; the revelation may be that there is no revelation. It is up to you. The onion man may be taken off kitchen duty and put on some other job detail where he cannot cry and simultaneously hide his tears. He may complain to himself of feeling all damned up and get into a fight as a result. He may break down, be ridiculed, or unexpectedly comforted. Or he may be put on garden detail and start planting onions instead of chopping them.

More indirect dialogue

* Write three different dialogues for two people about the weather. In David Mamet's *Duck Variations*, two old men meet in the park and ostensibly talk about the ducks; but they really discuss many different things. Mamet's dialogues are funny; see if you can get some humour into yours.
* Have two friends act your dialogue for you. As with your monologues, give them some director's notes. But also take note, yourself, of what seems unclear in your script, and correct it. When you and the actors are ready, tape the dialogues and listen to them. You may be surprised at what works and what does not. Play the tapes to other people and note their reactions.

Direct and indirect dialogue

* Write a direct dialogue between two people in a bank or at a bus stop.
* Now rewrite it in indirect dialogue. Have your actors perform the dialogues for you so that you can hear the differences. Sometimes very flat, realistic dialogue can be funny or, in a time of stress like a bereavement, for example, sad.
* Write a direct dialogue between two people choosing flowers at the florist's for a tribute to a dead friend, and a direct dialogue for a couple deciding to break up.
* Now write both in indirect dialogue. The same two people are skirting around the issues of flowers, death and endings.
* Now try a combination of the two – this is what most dialogues turn out to be. The indirect dialogue might come first, building tension, then leading to some sharp, direct exchanges. Have a look at the dialogue section in Chapter 8, 'Writing for stage'.

STRUCTURE

Chapter 7, 'Writing for screen and television', gives you a breakdown of the three-act plot. You may not wish to structure your play this tightly, but you need to know how structure works. Particularly on radio, where you are leading the listener blind through the action and dialogue, you need to develop your play coherently.

A writer must get in touch with the reader by putting before him something which he recognises, and therefore stimulates his imagination, and makes him willing to co-operate in the far more difficult business of intimacy. And it is of the highest importance that this common meeting-place should be reached easily, almost instinctively, in the dark, with one's eyes shut.

Woolf (1950)

Virginia Woolf is talking about writing on the page, but her words also apply to radio. By strengthening and clarifying the play, structure makes the listener feel safe – not too safe, but enough to venture into imaginative space with you. Conflict is the core of drama, and all plays need a protagonist – a central character – and an antagonist to oppose them. Actors are told to think in terms of verbs, not adjectives – in other words, to understand and define their characters in terms of what they do, or want to do. The word *want* is very important. According to the great director and theoretician Stanislavski, desire is the essence of theatre. Desire is what moves characters to action.

Macbeth

⁕ Read, or reread, *Macbeth*, and if possible listen to it on tape. You will only need Shakespeare's words to imagine Banquo's ghost, or the sleepwalking scene where Lady Macbeth repeatedly washes her hands. What you hear in *Macbeth* is what all plays must include: some kind of setting-up or establishing scene, a disturbance leading to a climax, and some kind of resolution.

⁕ Now find a copy, and a tape if possible, of a contemporary play such as Charlotte Keatley's *My Mother Said I Never Should*, which has been performed both in the theatre and on radio. What do the characters want? Do they know? Do they deceive themselves, like Macbeth? How honest are they and what do their lies – to themselves and each other – reveal about them? Your characters cannot always be nice, or they will not be real.

THE WHOLE PLAY

You may think of a plot which observes Aristotle's unities of time, space and action. Your play will happen on a single day, in a single setting, and the action of the play will dramatise one central story. But even Aristotle would probably have approved of flashbacks and flash-forwards if radio had existed in his time.

Imagine a play set on the day of your protagonist's funeral. It takes place in the home of the deceased, after the service. People are eating and drinking and revealing information constantly, but subtly. There are flashbacks to the service, and to scenes from the protagonist's lifetime. Start with a subdued hubbub, and people talking quietly and respectfully. The dead person could have been a musician who died of a drug overdose, or a young woman on a council estate who died of anorexia. Either character would have a whole cast of mourners.

Perhaps the protagonist had more than one partner, and the people concerned discover each other at the funeral. This could lead to conflict, humour or violence. Perhaps the anorexic woman was having an affair with another woman, which she was terrified to reveal. Perhaps the dead person was a female musician, or a male anorexic who was having an affair with a man, or wanted to.

You will need to flash back to various phases of the character's life. Try not to explain them or their death too neatly. The last act might return to the wake. We would listen to the comments of the mourners with much greater understanding. We would hear what they left out, or talked around.

You might want to use the dead person as a narrator, responding ironically to what they 'overhear'. They might criticise aspects of the occasion, including their mourners' outfits. The running commentary, providing a rich contrast to the events of the play, might be a *tour de force*. Your audience would be roped in, because who does not fantasise about their own funeral?

DRAFTING

When you have a draft of your play that feels as right as you can get it, try it with actors, and redraft on the basis of what you hear. Some cherished lines and speeches may have to go, whereas others you are not particularly proud of will work brilliantly. It is up to you to develop an ear for your own work, and be ruthlessly honest with yourself. Refer for help to Chapter 15, 'Redrafting and editing'.

Listen to the play again. You may need to tweak it rather than redraft it. When you are ready, direct and record it. Listen hard for weaknesses and strengths. You will find it thrilling to have actors say your dialogue, and will note that the lines change when spoken. You may need to have another tweak, or even write a further draft. Knowing when to stop is also something you learn from experience. Remember your timing. If your play is three hours long, it is unlikely to be broadcast.

MARKETING YOUR PLAY – THE SYNOPSIS

Selling a radio play takes persistence. Your work will be read faster by a local station than by the national BBC, who receive hundreds of scripts per month. First of all, find out if any of the local stations (such as BBC Radio Merseyside) offer slots for beginners. Try contacting them by phone. If you are encouraged to send in a play, always include a synopsis, and think hard about how to sell your idea. Fashions in synopsis writing change as markets change. BBC Radio Drama currently like an introductory sentence or two saying how the idea for the play came to you.

See if you can persuade a local station to let you into the studio to play around with effects and explore the medium's possibilities. You could also try hospital radio, which might welcome a short drama for patients, or even a soap. Even if you do not sell a finished play, you may make valuable contacts and receive valuable advice.

This is a time for your belief in your work to come to the fore. Never apologise for any aspect of it. Also remember that confidence is not the same thing as arrogance. You are proud of what you have written, and confident because it has gone through a long process of drafting and redrafting, of thought and improvisation and polishing. You are confident because of the process of writing itself. If you have followed all the steps, and not been self-indulgent about hanging on to favourite lines even when you can hear that they do not work, you are ready to summarise your work in a brief, positive way:

Synopsis of *Nursing Ambition*
Every little girl wants to be a nurse at some time or other. I certainly did, and I read about nurses in a series of books that made them seem glamorous and heroic – a hard combination to beat.

Sarah, the central character of *Nursing Ambition*, is a nurse, and having a disillusioning time of it. She too remembers the books about nurses she read as a child. The play opens with one such extract, exaggerated for comic effect:

Marsha knew the profession of nursing was a noble calling. She thought of Florence Nightingale, the brave, wonderful Lady with the Lamp. Could she ever be worthy to follow in her footsteps?

As the play goes on, Sarah herself is haunted by the ghost of Florence Nightingale. But the real Florence turns out to be even more disillusioned with her 'noble calling' than Sarah. The comic dialogue between these two grouchy, exhausted nurses illustrates what an underrated profession theirs has always been – in a humorous way.

The above is an example of how you might begin a synopsis. You would go on to outline the rest of the plot, with examples of dialogue. You would say where it was set. You would have researched the slots available in radio drama, and timed your play to fit into one of them.

When you have done everything you can to make your play work, it is up to forces beyond your control. Give yourself a rest. You may find your next idea starts to brew. Start making notes as you would for any piece of work … and so the process continues. Good luck and good listening.

10 WRITING A NOVEL

James Friel

GETTING STARTED

There is no one method of planning, drafting and completing a novel. The challenge will be in determining what habits, tricks and routines work best for you. What becomes most absorbing about writing a novel is discovering *how* to write it.

Some writers plan very little, if at all. They like the white heat of writing and inventing at the same time. This is as legitimate a way of working on a novel as any other, particularly if you are able to write every day, keeping your mind both fearless and focused. Some novelists draft a first page, revise it until it pleases, and continue in this painstaking way until the novel is completed. Others plan, prepare and brood for a long time before they even begin to write. In this way, they can concentrate not on *what* to write but *how*.

The ways to work on a novel are many. If you are new to the discipline it is easy to become overwhelmed by all the things a novel has to do, so do not deny yourself the pleasure of planning and dreaming your novel into existence. It can be the best part of writing one: so pleasant, in fact, that most people do not go beyond this point.

If, however, you are serious about committing yourself to writing a novel, then let it live in your head. Question it. Visualise it. Research it. Pull it apart. Dismiss it all as a bad idea and wait for it to come back. If it is an idea worth time, energy and thought, it will return – more fiercely than before.

A novel should demand to be written, even if you do not know why. Writing it will help you discover why. It needs to nag you to complete it and, in turn, you will have to nag it into completion. You are embarking on an intense and highly charged relationship.

Chapter 1, 'The writer's journal', is essential reading. Once you begin seriously to consider your novel, it might be a good idea to keep a special notebook devoted to it, or a file with separate sections for each chapter.

Title

Think of a title for your novel. It will help you settle on its main theme or intention. Let it be a working title. Be prepared to change it as the novel itself changes.

KEEPING GOING

The outline

An outline is a series of working notes that help you think about the events of the novel and how you want to arrange them.

Avoid writing a synopsis or a detailed treatment. If you can summarise your novel in ten neat pages of prose, why write three hundred more?

Here are some of Charles Dickens' working notes for *The Mystery of Edwin Drood*:

> *CHAPTER I*
> *THE DAWN*
> *Change title to THE DAWN.*
> > *Opium smoking and Jasper.*
> > > *Lead up to Cathedral.*
>
> > *CHAPTER II*
> > *A DEAN AND CHAPTER ALSO*
> *Cathedral and Cathedral Town*
> > *And the Dean.*
> > > *Uncle and Nephew.*
> > > > *Murder very far off.*
> *Edwin's story and Pussy.*
>
> > > *CHAPTER III*
> > *THE NUN'S HOUSE*
> *Still picturesque suggestions of Cathedral Town*
> *The Nun's House and the young couple's first love scene.*
>
> > > *CHAPTER IV*
> > > *MR SAPSEA*
> > *Connect Jasper with him. (He will want a solemn donkey by & by)*
> > *Epitaph brings them together, and*
> > *Brings Durdles with them.*
> *The keys.*   *Story Durdles.*
> *Bring in other young couple.*   *YES*
> > *Neville and Olympia Heyridge or Heyfort?*
> > *Neville and Helena landless.*
> *Mixture of Oriental blood – or – imperfectly acquired mixture in them. YES.*

The notes are sparse and personal. They make sense to Dickens. Your own notes could be more expansive and detailed but try to keep them rough, provisional, suggestive. This way you will be less precious about changing or discarding them. Notice, too, how Dickens' notes concentrate on action and character. Let these predominate in your outline.

I cannot guess at the story of your novel so here is a brief outline of a possible novel. It is adapted from a series of actual headlines and cuttings found in Paul Auster's memoir *The Invention of Solitude*.

i)   HARRY AUSTER KILLED
                  WIFE HELD BY POLICE
          Former Prominent Real Estate Operator is Shot to Death
                  in the Kitchen of the Home of His Wife
                  on Thursday Night Following a Family
                  Wrangle Over Money – and a Woman

ii)   WIFE SAYS HUSBAND WAS A SUICIDE

iii)   *Dead Man Had Bullet Wound in His Neck*
                  and in Left Hip and Wife Admits
                  That Revolver With Which the Shooting Was
                  Done Was Her Property – Nine-Year-Old Son,
          Witness of the Tragedy, May Hold Solution to the Mystery

iv)   ... *Auster and his wife had separated some time ago. An action for divorce was pending in the Circuit Court for Kenosha County. They had had troubles on several occasions over money ...*

v)   AUSTER SHOOTING:
                  WAS THERE 'ANOTHER WOMAN'?
... *Auster's widow told neighbours that her husband was 'friendly' with a young woman known to the wife as 'Fanny'. Neighbours heard the name 'Fanny' in the trouble between Auster and his wife immediately preceding the shooting ...*

vi)   WIDOW TEARLESS AT GRAVE
                  WHILE UNDER ARMED GUARD

vii)   ANNA AUSTER TRIED SUICIDE

viii)   ... *Anna Auster was released from the infirmary of the Kinosha County Jail into her brother-in-law's custody. Mr. Frederick Auster said he was convinced of his sister-in-law's innocence and both he and his wife, Annie, would take responsibility for the widow and her son ...*

ix)   FREDERICK AUSTER SHOOTS BROTHER'S WIDOW
                  NINE-YEAR-OLD SON MISSING

x)   MISSING BOY FOUND IN RAILWAY CARRIAGE
                  MILES FROM HOME

xi)   *BOY WEEPS AT MOTHER'S GRAVE WHILE*
        UNCLE WATCHES TEARLESS
        UNDER ARMED GUARD
xii)   *NEPHEW BREAKS DOWN IN COURT*
        AS UNCLE CONFESSES

The events are outlined in twelve points. There is, on the surface, a clarity and logic to these events but there are also questions that go unanswered, details that puzzle and contradict.

What has led to the killing of Harry Auster? What led to the break-down of the marriage? Money, we are told, and possibly another woman – but is this the truth? What is Auster's financial situation? Was Auster mean with money or was he short of it?

When I come to the first killing, I have to ask, did Mrs Auster really kill her husband? What was the nine-year-old son's involvement in the tragedy? Could the mother be covering up for the son? Why would so young a boy want to kill his father?

There is 'Fanny' to consider too, but is there any evidence she even exists? If she does, who is she? How did she meet Auster? Is she involved in Auster's finances? Does Frederick Auster know about her? What becomes of her in this story?

There is also the brother-in-law, Frederick, a late entrant in the plot. What is his story and how does it entwine with that of his brother and his wife? Can he be introduced earlier? What is his opinion of Anna and why, seemingly, does it change so radically and suddenly?

The questions are endless and the answers multiply, but throughout you are looking for symmetry in the way a story is told, unpleating the material to see how much there is.

Be prepared to invent, to improvise and test your theories, and dispose of them too if they do not work out. Let the material live in your head, expand, change and settle. Enjoy just thinking about it.

And trust the material to tell you things. At this stage your novel knows more about itself than you do. You have to listen to it. Be curious. Be patient.

Outline

Write an outline for your novel. Take your time. Concentrate on action at first – on what happens and why. *Never have a chapter without an event or action that moves the story on.* And remember that, while you plan, you are free to invent, to follow any line and then erase it.

FORESHADOWING

Your novel will always surprise you no matter how much you plan, but one advantage of working out the plot in advance is that you concentrate less on surprising yourself and more on surprising your reader, a far more artful and satisfying strategy.

For example, in the Auster plot you might want it to look as if the wife is the guilty party but let the reader suspect that the guilty party is either the son or Frederick. At the climax, however, you might reveal that the true culprit is 'Fanny' – the misheard name of Annie, Frederick's wife.

Did you forget about Annie?

In order to pull this off, you need to plant clues carefully as you go along, clues the reader fails to notice at the time but will recall when the revelation is made. You can only do this sort of thing if you know your plot, and where it is going, and that is another reason why planning your novel is advisable.

PLOTTING

Look again at the outline you are making of your novel. Are you telling a story? Does your outline have what the Auster plot has, what every novel needs and what your outline must also discover: a beginning, a middle and an end – a story?

In their chapters on writing short stories and screenplays both Jenny Newman and Dave Jackson make insightful comments on plot and structure that are just as pertinent to novel writing. If you reduce the whole question of plot and structure to its simplest form you come to see that *all* stories – short or long – begin with a disruption in the status quo. The normal flow of events is disturbed or complicated. A story follows the results of this disturbance, traces the consequences when something out of the ordinary occurs until a resolution is achieved.

One of Dan Rhodes' short fictions provides us with an example of this universal structure in miniature:

Tagged
When we started getting serious, I had my girlfriend electronically tagged. She thought this was terribly romantic, and whenever my radar device brought me to her work, the park, a café or a friend's house, she greeted me with a delighted smile and a long, gentle kiss. Lately I've started to worry that she's unwell. When I track her to the pool or the train she appears less surprised, her smile lacks its former dazzle, her kisses leave my cheeks much sooner than before. She seems distant and thoughtful. She really isn't herself. I think she should see a doctor.

Rhodes' story does not begin when boy meets girl – although it could. It begins when they 'started getting serious'. It is because of *this* that the narrator tags his girlfriend, and we follow the consequences of this decision until the resolution: the narrator thinks his girlfriend is sick and the reader thinks, no, *he* is! Dan Rhodes need take us no further.

The Auster plot outline is longer and more complicated than that of 'Tagged' but it follows the same formula of:

1. a disruption in the status quo
2. the consequences of that disruption until
3. a resolution is achieved.

Auster's murder is a powerful upsetting of the status quo. As a result Anna is arrested, attempts suicide, and is murdered by her brother-in-law. Her son runs away and the plot reaches a classic climax and resolution in a courtroom.

One of the flaws of an apprentice novel writer is starting the novel too early; an over-anxious desire to set the scene and establish the characters before the real action begins. The real action *is* your novel.

In your outline you must look for the event that disrupts the status quo. What begins the *real action* of your story?

In 'Tagged' Rhodes knows just where to begin and where to conclude. The Auster story could begin earlier with the Austers' marriage and the beginning of their financial troubles. You could go back to when they met or to Auster's childhood and his relationship with his brother; but isn't the story's real trigger that first shooting? Isn't this where the real action begins?

There are indeed novels – good ones – that begin slowly and reward a reader's patience, but ask yourself how many novels in your life have you begun to read and never finished because they failed to interest you early on. Do you want someone to do that with your novel?

POINT OF VIEW

Point of view or POV is about who is telling your story, from what angle or angles. Chapter 6 summarises the points of view most commonly used in short stories, and those descriptions apply to fiction of any length.

The first-person POV uses a narrator – one who can be outside or secondary to the main narrative – such as Lockwood in *Wuthering Heights* or Dr Watson in the *Sherlock Holmes* stories; or it could be the main character recalling past events – Holden Caulfield in J. D. Salinger's *The Catcher in The Rye; or* recreating them in a present-tense narrative, a stream of consciousness, or even in the form of letters or diaries.

A first-person POV can have an attractive immediacy but if, say, the son in the Auster plot were telling the story, there would be things that happened outside his range of knowledge, such as events before he was born. If you made Anna the first-person narrator you would have to face the fact that she dies before the narrative reaches its climax. You could tell the story from the point of view of Frederick but he does not witness his brother's shooting, for example. If your narrator does not witness the main or crucial events, this distances us from the action. This might make you over-reliant on the narrator being *told* things by other characters, which can look clumsy. You could, of course, use a multiple POV, using different narrators at key points.

The second-person POV is much more rarely used: Edna O'Brien's *A Pagan Place*, or Jay McInerney's *Bright Lights, Big City* are two of the few examples that come to mind. It is, perhaps, too powerful, too limited, too insistent a POV for an entire novel; but when you are plotting or drafting it can sometimes be a valuable exercise to write paragraphs from this POV if you are attempting to get into the mind of a character.

The third-person POV is more popular. A main character is described from the outside – Hemingway often adopts this POV – or subjectively, with the author relating the story through a central character or characters with access to their thoughts and feelings. The later novels of Henry James exemplify this approach, particularly *What Maisie Knew*. Again, you can use multiple third-person points of view too.

Whichever you adopt, you need to ask, even if this is the easiest way to tell your story, is it the best?

There is also the POV often referred to as 'third-person omniscient' because of its God-like gaze, the author having access to all the characters' thoughts and feelings, intervening to supply information and comment on the characters and their actions. This is a POV commonly adopted by Victorian novelists such as Dickens or George Eliot. It works well in complex plots or ones that range in space and time.

There are also combinations of all these points of view. A novel like Carol Shields' *Mary Swann* is in five sections. The first is in first-person, and the next two are in the third-person POV, as is the next but that one also uses letters and diaries, and the novel's final section is written in the form of a film script. A novel like Louis de Bernière's *Captain Corelli's Mandolin* also uses a variety of POVs to tell its story. This approach allows and encourages you to adopt a variety of styles too.

You need to experiment with these points of view but you also have to negotiate with your material as to which is the best to adopt. Whichever point of view you choose, be consistent. For example, to tell the Auster story from the son's POV and have the action filtered through him is one thing, but then dipping into the mother's POV for a paragraph here and there just looks clumsy.

BEGINNINGS (AND ENDINGS, TOO)

In his excellent book, *The Fiction Writer's Workshop*, Josip Novakovich lists various ways to start a novel. What follows are some famous examples:

Setting the scene

On the pleasant shore of the French Riviera, about half way between Marseilles and the Italian border, stands a large proud, rose-coloured hotel. Deferential palms cool its flushed façade, and before it stretches a short dazzling beach. Lately it has become a summer resort of notable and fashionable people; a decade ago it was almost deserted after its English clientele went north in April. Now, many bungalows cluster near it, but when this story begins only the cupolas of a dozen old villas rotted like water lilies among the massed pines between the Gausse's Hôtel des Étrangers and Cannes, five miles away.

F. Scott Fitzgerald, *Tender is the Night*

A startling sentence or hook

Hale knew before he had been in Brighton three hours, that they meant to kill him.

Graham Greene, *Brighton Rock*

A direct address

I'm Jared, a ghost.

Douglas Coupland, *Girlfriend in a Coma*

An idea or general observation

All happy families resemble one another, each unhappy family is unhappy in its own way.

Leo Tolstoy, *Anna Karenina*

A character in action

That night he dreamt there was evil in the rock. So, such concepts still exist in dreams, was his first thought on waking, and careful not to disturb, he got up to write his report, for the room was full of light.

Tim Parks, *Shear*

Characters in conflict

Nuns go by as quiet as lust, and drunken men with sober eyes sing in the lobby of the Greek hotel. Rosemary Villanucci, our next-door friend who lives above her father's café, sits in a 1939 Buick eating bread and butter. She rolls down the window and tells my sister Frieda and me that we can't come in. We stare at her, wanting her bread, but more than that wanting to poke the arrogance of her eyes and smash the pride of ownership that curls her chewing mouth ...

Toni Morrison, The Bluest Eye

A summary

Once upon a time there lived in Berlin, Germany, a man called Albinus. He was rich, respectable, happy: one day he abandoned his wife for the sake of a youthful mistress; he loved; was not loved; and his life ended in disaster.

Vladimir Nabokov, Laughter in the Dark

Exercise

Begin to amplify your outline by including attempts at opening sentences and paragraphs – not only for your first chapter but for each of them.

This goes for endings of chapters, too.

In either case, your aim is to entice, to seduce, to encourage and provoke a reader to continue reading.

Look at a whole range of novels, not just those you most admire. Study and practise such openings (and endings, too). Try a variety of approaches. See what works. By amplifying your outline in this way, you will have for each chapter a way of beginning and something to work towards. You need not fear the blank page.

CHARACTERISATION

You must spend time – a great deal of time – thinking about your characters *and* relating what you decide about them to what the plot demands of them. Action comes out of character and character is revealed in action.

A husband should not leave a wife primarily because your plot demands it. Each character should have an inner motivation. In the

Auster plot you have at least two murders. If Anna killed her husband because he was unfaithful, you would have to make us believe *she* would do this. Not every wife would do so. What makes Anna react in this way? What is it in her nature, her past, her relationships not only with her husband but those around her that make the violence seem inevitable?

Characters

In your outline begin to amplify your characters.

Make a note of every character in each chapter and begin to plot their progress through the novel as a whole. Ask yourself in what ways they change and develop – or reveal they are different from how they were originally perceived.

Make notes, too, on their physical appearance, on characteristic actions, significant lines of dialogue, motivations. Make each character distinct. Avoid bland description and generalised terms such as *pretty, nice* or *fat.* You need only one sharp, distinguishing detail to make a character come alive for a reader.

Introduce characters with a flourish. Instead of telling us about them, show them, dramatise them. Give them something to do rather than something to think or remember. In a novel, action is the best means of creating character. Establish each as physically and immediately as you can.

Go for a walk and interview your character. Grill them about what they really think about other characters and why, about what is happening to them, even about events outside your novel but, more relevantly, ask them about their involvement in specific chapters. Even if you are not writing from their point of view, this technique can throw up angles and nuances that animate the scene and deepen the action, get them to speak to you, listen to the way they use language, and observe how they might use such and such a gesture to accompany a particular phrase.

DIALOGUE

Character is best revealed by action; but remember that dialogue is also action and a chief means of characterisation for many novelists.

We speak far too imprecisely and at too great a length to serve a novelist's purpose. In novels, dialogue is a *re-presentation* of what we say in life, an edited highlight that must sound faithful, real.

Conversation

Write down a conversation between two characters from your novel making up after a serious argument. Make it last for at least two sides of 750 words.

Now, set yourself this challenge. In a film script, a page, on average, takes a minute to film. You need your conversation but cannot afford to spend two minutes of screen-time on it. You must reduce it to 30 seconds – to at least a quarter – less if possible – yet the scene must still work.

A novelist can resort to reported speech, but that can be as distancing as exposition, so try to reduce the conversation to its essential.

Remember that dialogue accompanied by description of pause, gesture, physical detail can be very effective. Often we do not say what we mean and it is our bodies that betray our true intention.

In life, we often do not say what we think. Our language is coded. When we listen to others, we intuit, even if their words sound perfectly pleasant, even jovial, that they are angry with us or disappointed or just simply being hypocritical.

Study this exchange

A	You're late.
B	Sorry.
A	My car ran out of petrol.
B	Did it?
A	Has the film started?
B	Yes. Did you really want to see it?
A	Yes, of course.

Rewrite this exchange, indicating that:

- A is angry and B is lying
- A is secretly amused and B is genuinely apologetic
- Neither A nor B care either about being late or missing the film –
- they are just glad to be together.

The conversation should not be significantly longer than it is now. What you are looking for is the giveaway sign that reveals a character's true state of mind.

Read your dialogue aloud. In fact, read all your work aloud; tape it and go for a walk with it playing on a personal stereo. It is a good way of making it *other*, of becoming your own reader, of taking words off the page and into that private place inside a reader's head where all the best novels come alive.

Avoid too much *he said, she said* and do not overuse its variations such as *he questioned, she responded, he averred* … Use *he said, she said* constructions to avoid confusion and vary them only if you want to convey a shift in mood. Ask yourself if you need to add *she screamed*. Is it because your dialogue does not convey this in its own right? Look at how little direction a playwright gives as to how a line should be said.

PROGRESSING

Key scenes

Your outline should be quite detailed by now. You have considered openings of chapters and endings. You have notes on character, lines of dialogue. If you have plotted your novel well you have a strong idea of where you are heading, but the end is a long way in sight. You have, however, key scenes to think about, important moments and events your novel needs to entice your reader along.

In the Auster plot, key scenes might be the ones in the graveyard as well as Anna's attempted suicide – which is the central event in the outline – and the courtroom scene with which the plot climaxes.

These scenes correspond to the three-act structure described in Chapter 7, 'Writing for screen and television'.

You should be itching to write scenes like these. They will be challenging and crucial scenes – intimidating – but, despite the difficulties, the desire to get to them is what gives you the momentum to get through the novel.

If your outline lacks such scenes then you should seriously consider what is missing and why? If you do not want to get to these scenes, why should anyone want to read them?

If the scenes scare you or puzzle you, do not lose confidence. Some of the suggestions in the next sections will help you. For now, write the scene very sketchily in simple plot points and build it up as you go along, returning to it when something new or helpful strikes.

DRAFTING

Most first drafts are either under-written, over-written or, usually, both in varying proportions. It would be a surprise if they were not.

Do not judge your first draft too harshly – or yourself. A first draft is allowed to fail. So is a second, a third and a twentieth. The idea that your prose should immediately stand to shiny attention is unreasonable and self-defeating. Its very imperfections are actually invitations to know it more deeply, to engage with it. It does not have to be perfect until it is finished – and sometimes not even then.

Remember, your first drafts are allowed to be messy, sketchy and inadequate. Try simply copying a draft out afresh. It may seem laborious but this is what redrafting is: quiet, long, patient work.

ANIMATING PROSE

Every now and then, when drafting, try writing each sentence separately, leaving a line on each side of it. This allows you to look at each sentence, see how long it is, how rhythmic, or, even, how necessary it is – and the space around it allows you to rewrite and fiddle with it. This practice will also alert you to the sentence as a thing in itself. Prose has rhythms, metre and variety just as poetry does, and a novelist must not be deaf to them. As John Gardner puts it:

> Prose like poetry, is built of rhythms and rhythmic variations.
> Like poetry, prose has rhythms and rhythmic variations.
> Rhythm and variation are as basic to prose as to poetry.
> All prose must force rhythms, just like verse.

Play with each sentence. See what sounds it contains. This may lead you into some fine, lapidary writing but remember, too, that prose can work by being seemingly careless. In prose, Thomas Hardy noted, inexact rhymes and rhythms now and then can be more pleasing and effective.

EXPRESSING YOUR THEME

You are drawn to write, often, because you have something to say. There is an opinion you want to express, a theme you want to explore, but novels tend to become wooden and strident when the attitudes are too evident. In the best novels, stories predominate over arguments, and characters are stronger than ideas.

In *Animal Farm*, Orwell argues powerfully against the evils of totalitarianism and he persuades us not by overt argument but by making us care for the animals that are abused and despise the pigs that abuse them; and by giving us a story that is fleetly paced and eventful. Character and action predominate. The ideas impress us because the characters are convincing and the action fluent and involving. It is not a great novel because it is a powerful statement of ideas; it is a powerful statement of ideas because it is, first and foremost, a sustained and moving novel.

This does not mean that you cannot 'think' in a novel, make statements, investigate concepts; rather you must do so subtly through characters and action that suggest rather than state openly what you want to say. The payoff is that, as a result, ideas become richer and more complex.

Identify your intention in a novel as a whole and a scene in particular. You may have more than one – you will have – so what is the main thing you want to communicate? Carol Clewlow says you should ask yourself, 'What is the one thing you want to do in a scene?' and then concentrate on just doing that – the rest will follow if you let it.

Perversely, having identified your intention, you will try to illustrate it with great restraint – not so much disguise it as imply it. Stendhal said, 'Find out what you most want to say and then try very hard not to say it.' Writing with a secret agenda gives a prose a pulse – a hidden but very real sense of animation.

Description

John Gardner (1984) describes an exercise in which you are asked to describe a barn as seen by a man whose son has just been killed in a war. Do not, he says, mention the son or the war or death. 'If worked hard enough, a wonderful image will be evoked, a real barn would stand before us but one filled with mysterious meaning.'

Try this exercise or another of Gardner's suggestions: a lake as seen by a young man who has murdered his girlfriend. Do not mention the murder. Or the girl.

Or find episodes in your novel which describe a place, imbuing it with unstated power.

A supreme (and concise) example of this comes from F. Scott Fitzgerald's *The Great Gatsby* at that point when, deserted by the woman around whom he has built a fantasy world, Gatsby floats in his swimming pool waiting for her call. It will never come. Instead it is his assassin who approaches through the trees. The narrator tells us at this point that Gatsby

… must have felt that he had lost the old world, paid a high price for living too long with a single dream. He must have looked up at an unfamiliar sky through frightening leaves and shivered as he found what a grotesque thing a rose is and how raw the sunlight was upon the scarcely created grass. A new world, material without being real, where poor ghosts, breathing dreams like air, drifted fortuitously about … like that ashen, fantastic figure gliding towards him through the amorphous trees.

That figure, his murderer, is the last thing Gatsby sees as he wakes from a dream existence into the nightmare of this one. Another writer, A. S. Byatt, in her novel *The Whistling Woman*, has a character realise 'the full force of the achieved simplicity in that perfectly created paragraph'. The adjectives – *unfamiliar, frightening, raw, scarcely created* – are both surprising and wholly apt. They suggest how horrifying Gatsby would have found his new reality. It is the end of Gatsby's ambitions and the moment of his death. This, short though it is, is a key scene in Fitzgerald's novel and his theme determines every word.

If you were to write the novel suggested by the Auster killings your main theme might be, say, to show how people are imprisoned by relationships. You have other things to say and to do in a scene – establish character, move the story on, describe the wallpaper – but if you keep your main intention firmly and uppermost in mind you know in that first scene – the shooting of Harry Auster – you most want to give an example of a family who once loved each other but are now trapped into hating each other. What you then choose to say about them, what you choose to have them say to each other, will be coloured by this intention, this theme of imprisonment. You will look at the house in which the killing takes place, how the moonlight comes through the blinds and stripes the walls like prison bars, how Anna's tight corset makes her feel, what it must be like to be a small boy – perhaps hiding inside a cupboard – watching his parents argue and be unable to do anything about it, and Auster realising his chief crime is that he does not love his wife and death is to be his punishment.

THE HABIT OF WORK

The idea for a novel can come like a Pentecostal flame but, while inspiration is powerful, it is also short-lived. It can drive you to start a novel but it will not sustain you through the long age it can take to complete one.

It is possible to write a poem that satisfies in one sitting. A short story might move from an idea to a finished piece with pleasing rapidity, but novels take time to write, a great deal of time.

No novel was ever written in an afternoon.

The difference between the many people who would like to write a novel and the few people who actually do is very simple: the latter find within themselves the discipline to work, and they work at being disciplined: they develop the habit of work. You need to be one of these people. You must learn to acquire discipline – the habit of work – to carve out that slice of time in which your novel gets written.

There will always be demands on your time from family, friends and your own desire for leisure, and so when writing a novel you must make more time, steal time, use the little time your life allows you.

1. Set aside a time when you can write and keep to it. Dorothea Brande in *Becoming a Writer* calls this 'making an appointment with yourself'. The phrase is a good one. It suggests you are important and so is what you are doing. Whatever time you can manage, make it as regular and frequent as possible.

2. Advertise this time to others who might intrude. Family and friends may try to interrupt – they may even mock at first – but what you are doing is difficult and demanding, and they need to realise that. When they see that you are committing your time in a serious way – when they see that *you* are serious – most people will come to respect your routine.

3. Stick to the appointment you make. As time goes on this will become easier. You will come to need this time, and insist upon it.

4. Stick to this time even – and especially – if no writing is achieved. It is dispiriting to sit and fail to produce anything worthwhile but, for now, keeping the appointment is more important than actually writing. You are developing a muscle that will make you a stronger and more disciplined writer.

5. Do not make the situation in which you can work – the house must be empty, the paper must be yellow and unlined, the ink must be blue – too demanding. It will become a means to prevaricate, a way of *not* writing.

6. Minimise distractions. Music, pleasant views, interesting books may create an atmosphere and may initially stimulate, but in time they might distract you. If you must have something, have a board pinned with images relevant to your novel. Don DeLillo keeps a picture of a stern-looking Jorge Luis Borges in front of him – 'a writer who did not waste time at the window or anywhere else'.

7. John Steinbeck would advise you to abandon the idea you are ever going to finish and, instead, plan to write a page a day. This is good advice in that it encourages discipline but does not allow you to be overwhelmed by all that you have yet to do.

8. Joyce Carol Oates observed, 'One must be pitiless about this matter of "mood". In a sense, the writing will create the mood.' Trust this to be true.

9. When you begin each session, reread what you wrote in the previous session. It helps to get you back into the rhythm of writing.

10. Do not worry too much about repetitious words, phrases or images. Until you are deeper in your written world you may not be able to judge or understand every detail your writing throws up, its import or its necessity – that comes with rewriting when you will hold every word, sentence, image and idea up to the light. Work by intuition. Trust the tale.

11. Trust your work to have its own energy, will, momentum, secrets. It is for this reason alone I suggest you go at your first draft free-fall, free-style. Avoid correcting or rewriting until the end of either each chapter or section or when the whole thing is down in one draft. Feel the flow. Respond to its rhythm.

12. Outside the time especially devoted to your novel, use your journal whenever you can. Every entry you make about your novel is a way of keeping you connected to it. Even when not writing, you are carrying it around in your head, and your head can barely contain it. A journal catches what might fall or be forgotten.

REVISING

You may be the kind of writer who revises as they go along or who writes one draft and then revises it. It is rare indeed for a novel not to undergo many redrafts. Here are some things for you to bear in mind as you redraft and revise your work:

1. When you are ready to face it, take out the first draft and read it. Just read it. Read the first draft without comment or addition – no matter how your hands itch to correct it and your head aches at the experience. Do not charge in. See what is there.

2. If you use a word-processor, print off a hard copy and read that. The screen with its neat fonts and straight rows can be very deceptive. Besides, this is closer to how your reader will experience your work. You need to know this experience, too.

3. Put it aside for a while. Let it brew. D. H. Lawrence would often keep his first draft in a desk drawer and refer to it only occasionally while he rewrote from memory. William Carlos Williams' advice was to put the draft away until 'the conditions under which it was written' are forgotten. 'In the meantime you become a different person, you become other than the person who wrote it and can judge it more objectively.'

   You might consider this relaxed attitude unwise, but where is the rush? Time spent on a book, Anthony Burgess observed, is of no real concern to a reader. If a first draft was written in white heat, let it cool down before you handle it.

4. Ask questions. All the time. *Is this what I want? What is it I want? Does this work? Am I trying too hard?* Remember this is not an exam. There are no right answers and you may take refuge in retaining a certain amount of ignorance. It is important to know what your intentions are in a work, but too much knowledge can be prohibitive. If you can summarise your intentions succinctly, why bother with the elaborate disguise of a novel?

5. There may be great changes to be made. Salman Rushdie's first draft of *Midnight's Children* was 900 pages long and written in the third person. Just one of his decisions on redrafting – to adopt a first-person narrator – meant every sentence had to be changed.

6. Be prepared – and brave enough – to make such enormous changes as well as small ones. If a scene bogs you down, move on to another. Let your unconscious mind solve problems, too. Move to something you can solve. The novel is always at work in your mind even when, physically, you are far away from it. The answer might come to you three days later on top of a bus or in the bath. It may be that the scene troubling you does not belong in the novel at all and its intractability is its only way of letting you know this.

7. Sometimes it is not your work that is tired and inadequate, it is you. You are human. This happens. The text is all potential. It wants to be realised, perfected. Leave it a while and return to it in a more belligerent mood. That said, it is often when one is most disenchanted that one makes the most merciless cuts.

8. Look at *all* your adjectives. Think of them as valuable coins. Spend them wisely. Do not waste them. A table that is *old, wooden, scratched* and *pine* is no longer a table, it is a list. The table is lost from view.

9. A man who *runs quickly* is a weak verb and a weak adverb. Why not have him *pelt, dash, race* or *rush*? Look at anything that ends in *ly* and consider saying goodbye to it.

10. If in doubt, leave it out. If a word, a phrase, a paragraph, a chapter really belongs, it will find its way back. You might think it easier to slaughter a particularly admired phrase if, instead of abandoning it altogether, you record it in your journal for later use, building up a private thesaurus of good lines that have yet to find their true home.

11. Is your work correctly punctuated? Punctuation is the breath of language – vital to a writer if you are to make sense, vital to readers if they are to understand exactly what you intend. To spend weeks, months, years on a novel and not endeavour to make it as accurate as possible is madness, laziness, simply ungenerous.

12. Use technology. Most word-processors have grammar checks – you might find them hateful and you can dismiss what they throw up, but at the very least it is a neutral – if insensitive – judge of what you have written.

13. Or have a friend read your work for grammar, spelling and punctuation. Friends will be much more helpful and more willing to comment about such things than about your work's literary worth.

14. Watch out for any confusions of singular and plural, and also tenses. Such errors need the most careful checking. You must be prepared to groom your drafts with absolute care and discrimination. In dialogue tense changes occur naturally. In exposition they look clumsy and can confuse.

When do you stop redrafting? Trust me. You will know.

Throughout this process you have been responding to your novel, trying to figure out what you need to do to make it work, to make it independent of you. A moment will come when the text will shrivel away from you, tired of your attentions, and say, 'Enough now. I'll do as I am.' Look forward to that moment.

Part Three: Branching out

11 SONG LYRIC WRITING

Dave Jackson

There are no rules to song writing. As soon as you try to say songs are this or songs are that, someone writes a song that breaks the mould.

COMMUNICATION

Like any other area of creative writing, song lyric writing is first and foremost about communication. What the lyricist wants to communicate will differ from writer to writer and song to song. Some politically motivated singer/songwriters feel obliged to use their creativity to try and change the world. To them, the generic love song disguises its true nature. Others would not dream of writing a song that did not tell a tale of new love found or old love lost. And others like to tell us horror stories or write slice-of-life mini-dramas. Then there are those songs which, if you take the lyrics at face value, mean nothing, but in the context of the music and the way they are sung seem to tap into something mythic.

The audience for songs is just as diverse. Some people are very word-orientated and will follow song writing which places heavy emphasis on language, but most people are not, and seem just to hear an overall soundscape.

Favourite lyrics

Think about your favourite song lyrics. Why do they appeal to you? Is it their clever word-play? Or the simplicity of their sentiments or ideas? Do the words intrigue or mystify you? Do they blend with the music or work against it, drawing attention to themselves as lyrics? Do the lyrics tell a story? Do they open up a new world or a different perspective on the world? Do they seem to speak to you directly? Do they affect you emotionally? If so, how?

Think about the type of songs you like and the type of lyrics you would like to write. Make some notes. Different writers have different ideas on what works best. Some lyricists trust their first inspiration and believe in getting a song written as quickly as possible. Others, like Leonard Cohen, will labour over certain songs for months or even years.

WHAT TO WRITE

Some songwriters seem to write solely from personal experience, about things that have happened to them – often unrequited love. Others find writing about themselves is too personal or too subjective.

It is probably best to be as flexible as possible. Try writing short rhyming stories about incidents or people you know or have read about. Write from different characters' perspectives. Randy Newman, for instance, always writes in the first person but in the voice of an adopted persona, usually an 'untrustworthy narrator'. You can always sneak bits of confessional stuff into your songs and pretend they are about someone else. I know a writer who sits in front of the television, making notes of images and things that were said, looking for random connections, chance meetings that would act as a source of inspiration. Films, novels, poetry, comics, paintings, photographs, computer games – anything can spark an idea.

Some writers approach lyric writing as an act of discovery. Rather than know what the song is going to say in advance and methodically plotting it, they develop the song from a few key words or phrases, using the metre of the melody line to give it forward motion. Sometimes serendipity can be the spark point for an idea. One contemporary song-writer tells a story of how he was in a pub when a guitarist from his band arrived. The guitarist told him he'd just been to see the French film, *Manon des Sources*. His French pronunciation, however, left much to be desired. The songwriter could not help asking, 'Man on the sauce? Is it about a heavy drinker?' He decided to write a song called 'Man on the Sauce.' As soon as the guitarist presented him with a riff to base the vocal on the lyrics seemed to write themselves.

Picking a subject

From the notes you made earlier, pick a subject for a song. Write a page of prose on that subject. Sort out the bits you want to make into a song. Pick an existing song that you know well, and using its melody, metre and rhyming structure write a new set of lyrics for it from your subject matter.

As you continue to write songs you should always be reacting and making corrections to your last piece of writing. In this way you will start to develop an awareness and a style. Some songs can be abstract and others very precise, some dreamlike, others gritty and down to earth. You can even contrast the one with the other within the same song, for instance with a gritty verse balanced by a surreal chorus.

Listen

You should listen to lots of different types of song. Listen to as much current music as you can, but also listen to old standards, like the cleverly crafted songs of Cole Porter, Oscar Hammerstein and Sammy Cahn. Listen to the blues of Robert Johnson and Willie Dixon, the country music of Hank Williams and the Louvin Brothers, or folk like the music of Woody Guthrie and Pete Seeger. Listen to Hal David's lyrical collaborations with Burt Bacharach like 'Alfie' and 'Walk on By'. Listen to Leonard Cohen, Bob Dylan and the Beatles. Listen to the different ways these writers make their lyrics work.

SING

Always sing your lyrics aloud. It does not matter if you have got the worst voice in the world; you need to sing the words to see if they work. Some words or lines that seem to work on paper may be difficult to sing. Do you allow the singer room to breathe?

Metre is easier to find when you sing songs aloud. Many lyricists do not have to think about what they are doing. The process seems instinctive, like talking. What we tend to forget is that we had to learn to talk. Learn to sing. Reread Chapter 4 on 'Rhythm'. Sing other people's songs and find the stressed syllables that make up the metre. Sing your own compositions in comparison. Be honest with yourself. How do they compare?

Sing while you are walking. Walking has been a source of inspiration to lyricists as diverse as Pete Townsend and Oscar Hammerstein. The rhythm and forward motion seem suited to the activity of songwriting. Sing in the car. It is useful to learn your own songs by rote, especially if you are going to perform them yourself.

TUNES

If you write your own music this obviously makes writing lyrics easier. Having the tune to hand or even just in your head is important. The melody and rhythm dictate the metre of the lyrics. You do not have to be a musician to write song lyrics. But non-musicians need to collaborate with musicians.

Some lyricists try to cram their words into the structure of unsuitable tunes. If you are not writing the music yourself, work closely with your collaborator(s). The musician might write a melody line for your lyric to follow. Alternatively you may improvise vocal lines to a guitar riff or a keyboard line. It helps to have a melodic or rhythmic structure to build your lyrics around. You may prefer to tape the music and take it away to try out different sets of lyrics and vocal lines in private. You may also want to try making up your own vocal melodies. You can then sing the finished lyrics to a patient musician or musicians who will dutifully work out the chords.

TITLES AND THEMES

Many songwriters recommend finding a title first and using it to work out the theme ('Man on the Sauce' being a case in point). Others start with a theme and let the title emerge with the song.

A generally accepted principle, however, is that individual songs should be about one subject, theme or concept. The most popular songs seem to be about fairly universal themes such as love. The trick is to approach the subject from a fresh angle.

A song I admire by Smog is called 'Ex-Con'. It is not actually about an ex-con but someone who feels like one when he puts on a tie to meet his girlfriend's family. The title acts as a plant which pays off within the body of the song. It has been said that you can sum up the theme or a story of a good song in a few words.

REPETITION OF KEY WORDS, VERSES AND CHORUSES

Many songs have what is known as a hook. This is usually a short phrase which has a rhythmic beat or idea which is repeated. Look for elements in the words that can be repeated – a chorus, an important verse or a line. A lot of songs repeat the title several times. Give people something to remember even after one hearing. You are trying to hypnotise your audience and draw them into your own little 3–5 minute world, and repetition is an effective way. As a rule, it is advisable not to make a song too long. Even I sometimes drift off a couple of minutes into 'Sad-eyed Lady of the Lowlands'. Try and grab the listener's attention in the first few words. You only have a very limited time.

DETAIL

Being specific about detail lends your writing a sense of authenticity. Rather than just singing about a man or a woman, give them a name. Say what type of expensive car you want the Lord to buy you. Tell us that you met her at 'St Martin's College' or focus on her 'Leopard-skin Pillbox Hat'.

CLICHÉS

Clichés and obvious rhymes abound in popular song. Sometimes the use of a cliché in an otherwise original lyric can be quite effective. Greg Milton came up with an effective inversion of two clichés in his song 'House by the Airport'. This song, detailing the collapse of a marriage, first talks about the husband having a 'sense of doing something right for the girl' but later drily mentions that 'He had a foot in every pie and a finger in every door'.

Many song titles are clichés ('Accidents will happen'), sometimes twisted for effect. Some become clichés ('The times they are a-changin''). However, if you fill your songs with too many of them, you run the risk of sounding banal and absurd.

OBVIOUS RHYMES

Often, when you listen to songs for the first time you are able to anticipate the next line. Sometimes the obviousness can be used to good effect, in order to go against the lyric's grain. But more often lyricists put in a line that rhymes simply to finish the song. This gives it an aura of triteness and inaccuracy which may ruin what may otherwise be a powerful lyric. Obvious rhymes are clichés too: try not to overdo them. Jonathan Richman uses a technique whereby he sets the listener up to expect an obvious rhyme and then does not rhyme the next line at all. This, sparingly used, can be quite effective.

It can be difficult to consider lyrics in isolation from the tune. The real danger for songwriters lies in combining all the elements of unoriginality. Writers of folk songs, for instance, may claim that although their songs may not have very original tunes, they are saved by effective lyrics. Many songs, loved by millions, have trite lyrics with many obvious rhymes but such an interesting or effective tune, melody or rhythm that this does not appear to matter, and the song becomes popular.

Even with all the clichés combined, the performance or production of a song can make all the difference. Some extremely original songwriters do not know how to present their work and fail to inspire much interest. Others perform their trite material so well they can hold an audience spellbound. How else do you account for Robbie Williams?

12 TRAVEL WRITING
Aileen La Tourette

> Since God first created man no Christian, Pagan, Tartar, Indian or person of any other race has explored every part of the world as thoroughly as Marco Polo, nor seen so many of its wonders. He himself thought it would be wrong not to keep a record of the marvellous things he had seen and heard so that people who knew nothing about them could learn from the book.
>
> *Bellonci (1984)*

INTRODUCTION

Travel writing has taken off in our time – pun intended. We might say that today people travel more for leisure and relaxation than out of necessity, or to go on a pilgrimage to a sacred site. But our reasons for travel also resemble our ancestors'. We, like them, travel in order to satisfy the craving, the restlessness, that sent explorers across uncharted seas. Early Christian pilgrims visited shrines in order to do penance, but often enjoyed their journeys so much that their church began to frown on them.

We have many different forms of pilgrimage, secular as well as sacred. People travel to Graceland in Tennessee, to Brontë country in Yorkshire, to Père Lachaise cemetery in Paris, to pay homage to figures from the past or leave tokens of their esteem. Travelling to a site which is special to us seems to satisfy a human need, as does telling each other our adventures along the way: think of Chaucer's *Canterbury Tales*.

Another kind of pilgrimage is a memory journey. Someone may travel to the country of their ancestors, or to a place where they once lived themselves. People travel to war cemeteries to find graves that have personal significance for them, or perhaps to meditate on the sheer number of graves that have resulted from bloody human conflicts.

Personal pilgrimage

Write an account of a pilgrimage you have made. You probably did not call it that, or think of it that way, but that does not matter. It may have been to a football stadium or a restaurant. Write about the anticipation with which you began your journey. What was it that drew you to this particular place? See if you can untangle the roots of its fascination for you. What happened when you got there? Was it what you expected? Be truthful, and include all the details you can remember as clearly and specifically as you can.

HITTING THE ROAD

> '... the road is life.'
> *Jack Kerouac*

Everyone knows the Chinese saying, 'A journey of a thousand miles starts with a single step.' As travel writers, we start with the journey. In *The Old Patagonian Express*, Paul Theroux talks about setting off for his on a commuter train. He reflects on the difference between himself and the other travellers: namely that for him the train is the first stage of an adventure, while to commuters it is simply a shuttle to work. He is isolating a major factor in tourist travel, and one that helps to make it an enormous source of energy and recreation: travel offers a break from routine. Humans are creatures of habit, and quickly adjust to their surroundings. This trait has helped us survive, but it can also result in loss of awareness. If we just go through the motions and do not look around us, life becomes dull. Travel, and travel writing, help us to get out of our rut.

Bon voyage?

* Think about a car journey you might have taken with your parents and siblings, or a bus journey with lots of other children when you were much younger. Write about the fights that broke out in the back – or the front – the car-sickness or bus-sickness, the flat tyres. Think about the monotony and the hypnotism of long train journeys, the conversations with strangers, the silences, the conjectures you make about your fellow travellers. Do not forget to include titbits you may have overheard, or sights you might have seen in a bus station or from a window.

- Listen to the music of travel, songs about crossing America by Simon and Garfunckel, for example.
- Write about as many different kinds of travel as you can. Remember to include examples like donkey rides, even piggy-backs: we are talking about locomotion here and what it feels like. What was fun and what was scary? What was both?
- When you run out of forms of transport known to you – and think about that word *transport* and its various levels of meaning – try and imagine one that is unknown. What would it feel like to waft off in a hot-air balloon, or climb up into the air in a helicopter?
- Try to find an account of the exotic form of travel you have chosen, and see how it compares with your imaginary one.

WHEREVER YOU GO, THERE YOU ARE

The best travel writers take us on an inward journey as well as an outward. This does not mean that the author is always in the way, like someone who brings back an album of snapshots with their own figure always in the foreground, blocking the view. It simply means they filter everything through their personality and sensibilities, and the writing carries a flavour of their attitudes, their unique point of view. Often travel writers use a journal to take us along with them, and to keep a record of their travels. Journals are personal by definition. No one can cram in every single detail. The process of selection is both subjective and revealing. Refer to Chapter 1 to remind yourself how it works.

Travel writing is different from guidebooks. It is not reportage. That does not mean a travel writer is free to air prejudices – far from it. But it does mean that instead of pretending to be totally neutral like a camera – and even a camera has the photographer's eye behind it – the travel writer makes a feature of subjectivity. No two people ever see the same thing, however hard they look. Paint your own pictures in your travel writing, deliver your own impressions, without worrying about what you 'should' think.

No place like home

- Go on a journey down your street. Think about what you know and do not know about it, and about the other people who live there. Try to notice at least five things you have never noticed before. Travel and travel writing both make us look at things again (as all good writing should do). In order for this to happen, you, as travel writer, must learn to look at things around you in a fresh way.

◦   Now write a travel piece about your street. Show it to someone else who lives there, if you can, perhaps someone in your family, and see if they agree with your vision of their street or not. They may point out things you have missed, or question things you have included. You will put in what you think is important, what you feel makes the place you live in what it is. If your reader reacts to something you mention in your piece by saying, 'You know, I never noticed that', you will know you have succeeded.

Where am I?

Keep a travel journal for a week. Detail every journey you make. Include maps and illustrations, snapshots or sketches. Talk about the 'souvenirs' you bring back, like fluff from a carpet. Make the smallest, most banal or disgusting detail amusing and alive.

GETTING LOST

'We know all too well that few journeys are linear and predictable. Instead they swerve and turn, twist and double back, until we don't know if we are coming or going.'

Cousineau (1999)

The experience of losing our way is universal. When children get lost in supermarkets, in shopping centres, in parks and forests, the incident has a kind of mythic resonance, like travel itself. In myths the hero often sets out on a journey, a quest. In its course, he often gets lost. There must be a sign, a clue, a miracle to bring the quest to a joyful conclusion.

Whatever their quest, the traveller too can get lost. It may even be that this was part of the journey's purpose, that life had become a bit stale, a bit too 'found'. Tales of getting lost and then being found – which can also mean finding oneself – read like little fairytales, miniature myths inside travel writing.

Hide and seek

Bring to mind an experience you have had of getting lost. Try to re-live your panic. What did you do? Where were you? Remember how threatening your surroundings looked: being lost makes everything darker and bigger than it is. Were you cold or hot? Hungry? Tired? How did you react? Write your getting-lost story, concentrating on:

> * your sense impressions – everything you saw, heard, touched, tasted and felt while you were lost;
> * the atmosphere of the place you were in, both while you were lost and when you were found again. See how it changed for you when it was no longer threatening. Also be aware of how strange you feel to yourself when you are lost – as if you were no longer you.

GOING FURTHER

'The only aspect of our travels that is guaranteed to hold an audience is disaster.'

Gellhorn (1978)

The stories in the groundbreaking anthology *Fortune Hotel* are primarily about disastrous trips. The book describes itself as 'alternative travel writing' and is an antidote to traditional narratives in which travel is always exciting and exhilarating and 'adventure' is a much over-worked word. Likewise Anne Tyler's novel *The Accidental Tourist* uses a certain kind of travel as a symbol of an emotional condition. The central character writes guidebooks for business travellers. He tries to spare them as much hassle as possible, and ends by sparing them the experience of travel as well, just as he has arranged his own life in such a way as to spare himself the inconvenience of feeling.

In *The Snow Leopard*, the American writer Peter Matthiessen describes his journey into the Himalayas on a quest to see a beautiful and elusive animal, and meditates on aspects of his life while tracking it. He sometimes gets close to it, but never actually sees it, and begins to realise the significance of the journey itself and the reflections it has prompted, not in a sentimental, silver-lining way but in a real, felt way.

If you go back to the accounts of Marco Polo's travels, which you should, you will find rich descriptions of every kind of obstacle, not all of them overcome. The marvellous stories of Victorian women travellers are filled with details which emphasise the hazards of travel as well as the delights. Caryl Churchill uses Isabella Bird, one of the best known, as a character in her play *Top Girls*. Isabella Bird's speeches make us aware of the many ills she suffered, or thought she suffered, which makes it all the more amazing that she travelled as much and as intrepidly as she did. Her speeches also remind us of another motive for travel, besides restlessness and the desire to visit a place, a shrine or a person – sheer escapism.

P. J. O'Rourke's *Holidays in Hell* tells of visits to unlikely and unappealing places like Chernobyl, and Martha Gellhorn's *Travels with Myself and Another* is an earlier example of a travel book which is hilarious in its recital of woes. Bill Bryson's travel books are filled with wry accounts of disasters and near-disasters on the road, and Joseph O'Connor's *Sweet Liberty: Travels in Irish America* sets out to explore places in the United States with Irish names, only to discover that most inhabitants of such places are completely ignorant of their Irish heritage and totally indifferent to it.

Disasters

- Think of a disastrous journey of your own. It might be a romantic or family holiday that went wrong.
- List all the details that made it catastrophic.
- Now write about it, exaggerating rather than playing down the things you have listed. See how much more interesting it is than a cosy travel story where everything goes according to plan.

The important thing is not to be too high-minded about your disasters. If you got into a fight in a bar and ended up having to run for your life, say so. If you were drunk as a skunk at the time, tell us that too.

IN THE FOOTPRINTS OF ...

Another kind of travel writing involves following in the footprints of an earlier traveller. You are paying homage to the original traveller(s) and also giving yourself a particular kind of journey. You may feel intimately in touch with the person whose itinerary you follow. The poets Simon Armitage and Glyn Maxwell repeated the journey that W. H. Auden and Christopher Isherwood made to Iceland. They tell the story of their own journey and recap details of the original one in their book *Moon Country*. Alan Hankinson tracks Coleridge in *Coleridge Walks the Fells: A Lakeland Journey Retraced*. Sometimes these repeat journeys have a melancholic side, as the contemporary traveller faces a far more crowded landscape than the original traveller ever dreamt of or, even more seriously, detects signs and symptoms of ecological deterioration. Many travel books include details of the destruction of our planet and its inhabitants.

Follow the leader

- Find an account of a journey you particularly like the sound of, one that is not beyond your present geographical reach, but which belongs to another time. It could be an account from a piece of travel writing as such, or from fiction – a description of London by Dickens, for example.

⚬ Follow the footsteps of the character/travel writer and see if you can see what they saw. You may have to use your imagination if the place is entirely transformed.

⚬ Now write an account of your journey, detailing all the changes that have taken place since the original journey was made.

WHEN IN ROME …

Yet another kind of traveller goes into a community and lives its life for a time, or tries to. This is a demanding and engrossing form of travel, involving not only a physical journey but an attempt to become part of another culture. Examples of this kind of travel include *Mutant Message Down Under: A Woman's Journey into Dreamtime Australia* by Marla Morgan, and *Thank You and OK! An American Zen Failure in Japan* by David Chadwick. Both these authors attempt to live as one of the people he or she is visiting. Morgan describes a privileged period spent on walk-about with aborigines, and the enormous respect she felt for their way of life. Chadwick talks about Zen, his own struggles with it, and with Japan.

Fitting in

⚬ Think of a time when you had to assimilate with what was, to you, a foreign culture. It may be as simple and domestic as your attempts to 'fit in' when you first went to school.

⚬ Remember the strange signs you had to learn to interpret, and the new language. If you grew up in two different households, what adjustments did you have to make in each? If you have travelled as a student, or even gone to a foreign restaurant where you were confused by the menu, flavours and customs that surrounded you, you can write about these experiences. The main thing is not to assume that anyone is right or wrong. Simply tell us what it felt like to be the stranger, the one out of step, and how you coped – or not.

RELUCTANT VOYAGERS

Many people travel because they have no option. We can be forced to take journeys by sickness, hardship, sorrow, political change, natural catastrophes. We may be removed from the things that normally give us a sense of who we are – and from familiar people.

> **No choice**
>
> Think of a reluctant journey in your own life, maybe a journey to hospital or school. It must be one that involved you in a loss of control over your own days and nights. You may have had to wear special clothing or depend on a small supply which you brought with you. You may have been out of touch with people you were used to seeing, and not able to contact them, or only at certain times. Write an account of this sojourn, whatever it was, but clearly and precisely and without self-pity.

SELLING YOUR WORK

Many people want to be travel writers. The chief reward of the job is the opportunity to travel and be paid for it, so the competition is stiff. You will have to offer something original. I do not mean that you have to hang-glide your way around the world, or bungee-jump in every major city. But your point of view, your intent in setting out, will have to have a slant that interests an editor.

Do not be afraid to start with your local paper. There might be walks you can take around your area that an editor will publish, if you write them up interestingly enough. Include conversations with eccentric locals, especially elderly ones, with sprinklings of oral history and accounts of how things used to be.

You are unlikely to be handed a huge budget for expenses right away. Make use of all your travel opportunities. Try to find something other people have overlooked. Approach your destinations with humour, openness, a willingness to be astonished or disappointed or enthralled – or bored silly, as Martha Gellhorn was with Bali. Like all writing, travel writing demands that you be yourself – your worst self or your best, your most courageous or your most depraved. Human beings are endlessly curious about each other and the world. Make the most of that precious curiosity.

13 WRITING ON THE WEB

James Friel

INTRODUCTION

First, a confession: this chapter was drafted in longhand numerous times before it ever reached a computer.

You too may like the feel of pen and paper and much prefer it to keyboard and screen; but, in order for this chapter to reach my editors, I had to resort to a word-processor to store and make copies of it, to revise, edit and print it out before sending it as an email attachment.

Agents and publishers will only read work that has been word-processed. Your computer is an essential tool but it is more than a type-writer with a monitor: within it lies not only your future as a writer but also, perhaps, the future of writing itself.

READING AND THE WEB

John Gardner wrote that reading should feel like an uninterrupted dream. Errors in expression wake us from that dream, and so too do errors of fact. In writing, detail must be accurate and convincing, both plausible and surprising. Not all your readers will notice if your surgeon character picks up the wrong knife or know that an anaemic liver turns not pale pink, but paper white, but you must write as if they will.

Appendix B emphasises the importance of researching your writing, and cites the internet as a vast research tool, littered with quirky, exhaustive and original detail that might animate your work and so deepen the reader's dream – but you need to search for it.

SEARCH ENGINES

You will need a good search engine to navigate the internet's many sites and pages. Try:

Google   www.google.com
Ask Jeeves   www.ask.jeeves.com
Yahoo!   www.yahoo.com

You do not have to restrict yourself to one search engine. Some, like Yahoo!, have so large a directory you can be overwhelmed. Ask Jeeves encourages you to ask simple questions and Google arranges its results in terms of those pages most visited by others, and its clear layout is a boon to the novice surfer.

Whichever search engine you use, take the time to read its Help file before you begin. You will learn to express your query more succinctly as well as to use shortcuts, such as + and – symbols, and placing key phrases in quotation marks, which can help pinpoint more exactly the object of your enquiry.

ONLINE REFERENCES

The internet is vast, uncensored and unchecked. Not all the material you encounter will be valid, definitive or tasteful. Bear this in mind when you search out information, and check your sources. For this reason, you could also take advantage of online research material such as:

Bartleby Online Reference   http://www.bartleby.com/reference
Online Dictionary/Thesaurus   www.yourdictionary.com
Online Encyclopedia   www.encyclopedia.com

Even if you still prefer to research from books, you can also use a search engine to discover if your local library's catalogue is online, or access the catalogues of these national libraries:

The British Library   http://www.bl.uk
Library of Congress   http://catalog.loc.gov/

NEWSGROUPS

The web is global in its scope and range and can provide you with a community. Out there are people who know things you wish to discover and who may also have things to learn from you. You will find them in newsgroups.

Your search engine will find newsgroups on any subject; but a great number of them are on Usenet. Usenet is like an enormous billboard or newspaper divided into topics and subtopics. There are subjects as varied and general as science (alt.sci) or books (alt.books), or as specific as marine biology (gov.us.topic.nat-resources.marine) or ancient foods (rec.food.historic).

Once you subscribe to a newsgroup you can post questions ('What happened to Napoleon's horse?') and wait for someone to tell you ('Two of its hooves were turned into snuffboxes'), or suggest a site that will lead you nearer to the answer.

Newsgroups are particularly useful if you are interested in historical or science fiction where accurate and convincing detail is essential.

To access Usenet and its newsgroups you need to download free software (www.1reader.com), but your internet provider will also run newservers and you may already have MS Outlook Express that allows you to read News. Also, Google runs a web-based newsgroup directory that does not need software: (http://www.groups.google.com/)

You will find a very helpful and exhaustive directory of groups concerned with all forms of writing at www.excite.co.uk/directory/Arts/Writers-Resources. You will discover here not only links to agents and publishers but also groups devoted to genre fiction, poetry, song writing and screenwriting, as well as online workshops and tutorials.

WRITING AND THE WEB

The internet's world wide web is a medium, a means to express yourself, communicate with others and publish your work.

Most literary magazines now have online versions, but there are also many reputable and engaging web-based magazines and most of these allow you to submit your work by email or email attachment. For detailed but far from exhaustive directories of such magazines, access:

Excite Directory of Online Writing http://www.excite.co.uk/directory/Arts/Online_Writing/E-zines/Directories

The Council of Literary Magazines and Presses http://www.clmp.org

If you are considering submitting work to an online magazine, it is very important to do the following:

* Read the magazine's contents and editorial before you submit any work.
* Read its submission guidelines thoroughly. Some magazines accept work only of a certain length and only at certain times of the year.

If you do not do these things, you may be wasting not only your own time but also that of the people running the magazine.

Bear in mind that the web welcomes songwriters and filmmakers as well as writers of poetry and prose.

You may even consider publishing your work via the web in e-book form. E-books can be accessed on special hardware, CDRom or downloaded via email.

Some publishers, like Trafford (www.trafford.com) offer an 'on demand' publishing service in which your manuscript is turned into a bound book with an ISBN number and barcode so that it can be ordered through bookshops and libraries. Your book is made on demand and this cuts down storage costs and also means your book need never go out of print.

Royalties can be far higher than those offered by mainstream publishers, but bear in mind that the public, so far, has been very reluctant to buy e-books. You must check sites that offer these services carefully. Will you retain all the rights? Will they allow you to contact authors they have previously published?

Established writers need to lead the way here but even the bestselling writer Stephen King failed to make a financial success of his e-book. His commitment to the form, however, is telling. The e-book *is* on its way, but think carefully before you become one of its pioneers.

WRITING AND THE WEB

Online magazines and publishers offer you a platform for your work but realise, too, that on the web you can make your own platform.

BLOGGING

A blog is short for a weblog.

In appearance it is similar to a writer's journal or commonplace book: short entries arranged in chronological order, excerpts, quotations, commentaries and links to other blogs and websites.

Far easier to create, edit and update than a personal website, the blog has become in a very short time an immensely popular form – one which might be very appealing to you as a writer.

The novelist William Gibson, author of *Neuromancer*, keeps a regular blog (www.williamgibsonbooks.com) and this excerpt from it should you give you an idea of why he does so, as well as an idea of a typical writer's blog.

Like a magpie without a nest

That's how Rudy Rucker...described how it feels to be a novelist between books. No place to take the shiny things we constantly find ...

No place for the magpie mind to take the trinkets and bits of tinfoil, currently. If I bring them here, for instance, I'm just leaving them on your window-ledge, something no magpie would ever be satisfied with doing.

I've been using this blog to keep track of stuff that needs to work its way into my novels for years now. Rucker's blog is nothing but notes on his books. Sterling says you can extrapolate his next book from the links on his blog. I betcha that's true of Warren Ellis, too. Blogs are the new novelist's commonplace book. I've been saying this for a while, but I thought I might be the only one. Discuss.

The underlined words link you to the blogs and websites of his fellow writers and the last allows you to email the blogger with your own thoughts. These writers use blogs as ways of not only thinking aloud about their work but also of interacting with other writers and readers.

You can download software to create blogs but at the moment the leading site (www.blogger.com) allows you to have a web-based blog that is both free and without advertisements. In two minutes of visiting this inventive and appealing site you will have your own simple and stylish blog.

Chapter 1, 'The writer's journal', should give you plenty of ideas for content, but also use your blog to list website pages and articles and other blog entries you have come across and found stimulating.

The best blogs are purposeful, frequently updated, and tightly written with a strong sense of both personality and narrative. Most significantly, they interact with and comment on the blogs of other writers. Like newsgroups they offer the solitary writer a community of like-minded friends with whom you can share your thoughts and your work.

YOUR OWN WEBSITE

Gibson's blog can be accessed through his website and it is increasingly common now for writers to have their own websites. For a sample of writers' websites, access: Authors on the Web at http://www.people.virginia.edu/~jbhauthor.html

If you are going to create a site of your own you should look at as many examples as you can and build up your own criteria as to what makes a good website.

Some of the sites you will access will have a very corporate look and be created and maintained entirely by the author's publisher. Some sites are maintained by enthusiasts and can vary in quality, but the best and most involving tend to be those maintained by the writers themselves.

William Gibson's is a good example but also look at the sites run by Michael Chabon (www.michaelchabon.com) or T. C. Boyle (http://www.tcboyle.com). Whether these writers are to your taste or not, each site conveys their styles well and gives a strong sense of what their work as a whole is like.

These are established writers with strong followings and, at the moment, you are probably not in the same position; so, you need to create a site that does more than inform the world of your existence. It should give a taste and feel of what kind of writer you are.

- Use your search engine to find sites of writers you like – or are most like!
- Study the design and content.
- Are the pages immediately clear, particularly the first page or home-page?
- Is the site easy to navigate or do you get lost, bored or easily distracted?
- What makes you stick to a site?
- What would your website look like?

This last question may be more difficult to answer than creating the site itself. What a website does is force you to consider what kind of writer you are. What is your public face? What colours, fonts, icons best convey you as writer?

Most computers come with software that allows you to create and design a homepage and website. Your internet provider will often encourage you to create one. You can often download the software freely from the net – try your search engine – and there are even companies which will design a website for you. It can be a difficult and time-consuming business but it can also reap considerable rewards.

Make the initial page or homepage neat and simple in its design, and keep text to a minimum. You will be tempted to use a riot of colours and may end up with a page that inspires only migraines.

Your homepage should have a list of contents so that its nature is immediately apparent. You can then link to excerpts from your writing, examples of works-in-progress, even an email link so others can contact you. You might even incorporate your blog, too.

Once your site is up and running, consider joining WebRing. This links your site to other similar sites and in this way increases traffic to your own. For a directory of WebRings related to writing, try WebRing Directory at http://k.webring.com/hub?ring+writingwebring

HYPERTEXT FICTION

Hypertext fiction is fiction that is aware of the world wide web, is created for the medium itself and exploits the differences between the page and the screen. Its main characteristic is its non-linear nature.

Think of a classic plot – boy meets girl, boy loses girl, boy finds girl. Even if you complicate the story – boy, having lost girl, thinks back to the time he met girl and, as he retraces the past, he finds her again – the events still unfold in time and the reader follows them in the order set down by the writer. Simply put, in a novel we begin at the beginning and read on until the end; or we read the first line of a poem, then the second and so on. We are guided, in each case, to a conclusion.

However, there have always been writers who have chafed at this chronological straitjacket. In John Fowles' *The French Lieutenant's Woman* the author makes frequent appearances, discusses possible plots and difficulties and, eventually, tossing a coin, gives us two alternative endings. In a previous century, William Thackeray has his amoral heroine Becky Sharp seem penitent and newly virtuous at the end of *Vanity Fair*, but the last thing on the printed page is Thackeray's own illustration that has Becky leering back at us and looking far from remorseful. Thackeray, first as writer and then as artist, gives us two distinct endings, deploying image and text in a way that anticipates hypertext fiction.

Other writers have gone further. Vladimir Nabokov in *Pale Fire* gives us a novel in the guise of a long poem with footnotes so that we do not read in a continuous sequence but flip back and forth between notes and poem which, more often than not, conflict with each other. Milorad Pavic's *The Dictionary of the Khazars* can only be read in the way one would read a dictionary or encyclopaedia, dipping back and forth between entries. There are even two published versions of the novel – one male, one female – but whichever edition is read, no two readers will experience the novel in the same way.

Readers of such texts are encouraged to become actively involved but, even when you read more conventional literature, do you always act passively in the face of a text? Think about your own reading habits, the way you might skip your way through a novel. Do you finish a novel in one sitting? Do you read every word? Do you ever flick forward to see what might happen or flick back to remind yourself of a certain scene or character?

Hypertext fictions develop this subversive approach to both writing and reading. They play games with the relationship between a text, a reader and a writer in new, fruitful and liberating ways. As will become apparent, the old distinctions of prose and poetry no longer hold quite true. In hypertext fiction the page is replaced by a four-dimensional space. It can incorporate animation, music and video. Familiar conventions become interestingly fluid and playful.

You do not need to be a computer expert to explore hypertext fiction. You need only to access the internet and you will find a vast new library waiting for you. You do not even need to be technologically adept to create hypertext fiction. You need only be able to link pages together. Creating a blog shows you how to do this and if you manage to compose your own website then you have ample skills to create hypertext fiction.

You create pages with blocks of text (and images and music too if you wish) and then link these spaces to create a narrative, determining where a reader can proceed within a work, blocking their progress, persuading them to go this way or that way but, crucially, always allowing a reader a choice, so that not only do the narrative possibilities multiply but a reader's power to determine them also multiplies. Point of view, closure, structure, time itself become playthings for the mutual pleasure of writer and reader.

Surf the internet and find examples of this new form of writing and telling stories. In particular, check out:

253	http://www.ryman-novel.com/
Hyperizons	http://www.duke.edu~mshumate/index.html
Intelligent Agent	http://www.intelligentagent.com
New River	http://ebbs.english.vt.edu/olp/newriver/
trAce	http://trace.ntu.ac.uk

If you fail to find these sites or any of the sites mentioned in this chapter – sites do go out of use or change addresses – try typing their titles in the text box of your search engine.

Hypertext fiction has proliferated at an amazing speed and this is one of the reasons why this chapter cannot be a definitive guide. Technology advances. Websites date or go out of use. New software appears with increasing regularity and the ways in which, as a writer, you can use the web increase with a similar rapidity. So this has been less an introduction to the subject and more an invitation to explore what may be the future for all of us involved in imaginative writing.

If you are inspired not only to read on but also to create hypertext fictions of your own, information about online workshops and courses can be found on several of the sites mentioned. You could also visit Eastgate directory at http://www.eastgate.co/Course.html

The dazzling combinations that are possible with hypertext fictions will provide you with new readers and new challenges. There is a virtual universe waiting for you. Explore, inhabit and enhance it.

14 WRITING FOR CHILDREN

Rose Flint and Jenny Newman

INTRODUCTION

The writer John Berger once said that he saw the story as a shelter, and imagined the storyteller sitting down with a cluster of listeners, coming in under the shelter of the story. Try and think back to the storyteller in your house, neighbourhood, school or library. If you are lucky, you will remember a voice: of a grandparent or teacher, or of a narrator on radio or television. That voice was telling you a bedtime story: a tale which settled you down and made sense of the teeming world.

Alison Lurie suggests in *Don't Tell the Grown-Ups* that many classic children's authors used fiction to find a childhood they never had, or recapture one snatched away from them. This does not mean that you as a children's author need to have had an unhappy childhood. But children's novelists engage with the child rather than the worldly-wise, compromised adults. You will need at least to rediscover the child in yourself, and set aside the layers of knowledge that can leave us authoritarian or cynical. Contemporary children's novelist Jacqueline Wilson said in a recent interview, 'Sometimes I upset adult readers because I write from the child's point of view about parents who let them down – I can see that that might be unsettling.' As Angela Carter says in her Introduction to *The Virago Book of Fairy Tales*, children's culture is an 'unofficial' culture.

AGE RANGE

Because stories for younger children involve collaboration with an illustrator, which lies outside the scope of this book, this chapter will focus on writing for children between eight and fourteen years. But knowing how publishers divide the children's book market may help you decide on your target age group.

- Washing-machine-proof fabric books introduce babies to the idea of reading. Their pages are robust and have characters who grunt, moo, rattle or squeak when a button is pressed.
- For older babies and toddlers there are board books with a simple narrative and laminated pages tough enough for readers first learning to turn them.
- Slightly older children will enjoy the pop-up books which often have lavish illustrations and a surprise on every page. For three- to six-year-olds there are mechanical books like *The Dragon Machine,* written by Helen Ward and illustrated by Wayne Anderson, in which the reader shares in the construction of a pair of mechanical dragon wings. Such books often use rhyme, rhythm and repetition. If you enjoy making word games and rhyming poems you may be drawn to writing for early years children.
- Younger fiction, aimed approximately at five- to eight-year-olds, is subdivided by reading ability: beginners, developers and capable readers. These novels are often illustrated and may run to 8,000 words. Writing for these categories is highly specialised and frequently commissioned.
- General fiction covers the eight to twelve age range. It includes series and stand-alone novels, and may run from 20–40,000 words, though longer books are sometimes accepted. Novels are strongly plotted, and their topics can be challenging and contemporary, as in Michael Morpurgo's *Out of the Ashes,* which looks at the foot-and-mouth crisis through the eyes of a young girl.
- Teen fiction also includes series as well as stand-alone novels, and can run to 60,000 words, with complex subplots and mentally and emotionally demanding subjects such as bullying, divorce, incest and terminal illness.
- Genre fiction covers a broad age range, and the *Who Next? Guide to Children's Authors,* edited by Norah Irwin and Lesley Cooper, breaks it down into 24 categories: Adventure, Animal, Ballet, Environment, Family, Fantasy, Ghost, Supernatural, Historical, Horror, Humour, Magic, Myth, Other Lands, Pony/Horse, Romance, School, Science Fiction, Social Issues, Space, Sport, Stage, Thrillers and War. Though these topics obviously cross over, the list is a useful way for publishers, bookshops and libraries to advertise and categorise; and knowing how your fiction might be perceived and marketed can help you focus. As is shown by Terry Pratchett's millions of readers, and the explosive success of J. K. Rowling's Harry Potter novels, fantasy is a current bestseller.

Even within the above categories, the demands made on the reader by language or content will differ from book to book. Simple, plot-driven narratives for the younger age range can involve rich characterisation and vocabulary; while a teenager who finds reading difficult still needs a novel with themes and emotions relevant to their age.

As a children's author you could begin by pondering the books you loved as a child. Recapturing how it felt to read them for the first time, evoking the thrill of anticipation and reliving the sensuousness of the experience, will help your own writing acquire a special resonance.

- Collect two or three books you remember with affection. Have your notebook to hand.
- Do you remember where you usually went to read? Was it comfy and snug or chilly and hard? Was reading a secret or open activity? Did you take a pet? Or something to eat?
- Try to recall what your life was like then. Who was your best friend? What was happening in your family? What were you looking forward to? Make a list of everything you remember.
- Now start browsing through the books. When a passage strikes a chord, make a note. It could be an episode you remember, or one that touches you for the first time.
- Taking that chord as a starting point, write for ten to fifteen minutes. Do not analyse, but do something dreamier, nearer to free-associating or improvising. See where it leads you.

THEMES

Stories have long been used to convey in a way accessible to young imaginations what the culture knows but the child does not – or only to a limited extent. Life can be uncertain beyond the home, so do not stray off the path or talk to strange men. Fiction can also look at dangers closer to hand. Many well-loved stories – such as Louisa Alcott's *Little Women* and J. M. Barrie's *Peter Pan* – invoke a loving and united home. But as novelist Hanif Kureishi has written, the happy family can be a dream or a nightmare. Children's fiction often revolves around points where it shifts from one to the other, and can incorporate lessons on how to foil or placate loved ones who change into frightening monsters. Even when the fictional home is stable, many popular stories waste no time in leaving it. Children, it seems, want out – at least in their fantasies – and escape provides a potent narrative structure.

Many protagonists take to the road, like Dick Whittington, or the rabbits in Richard Adams' *Watership Down*. Though your hero will need an aim (money, safety, the search for a lost parent) the usual subtext of such quests is the process of growing up – or refusing to. The ultimate boy hero may be Mark Twain's Huckleberry Finn, who rejects 'sivilisation' entirely, and is last seen lighting out for the world beyond the frontier. Young readers also love alternative families, which may explain the popularity of fictional boarding schools from Enid Blyton's Malory Towers to J. K. Rowling's Hogwarts. Hollow trees, thieves' kitchens, never-neverland: spend time devising a breathtaking new home, remembering that the most popular – like the pirate ships in R. L. Stevenson's *Kidnapped* or in Richard Hughes' *High Wind in Jamaica* – are often more uncomfortable and demanding than those left behind.

Today's novels for older children do not flinch from domestic problems. Anne Fine's *The Tulip Touch* takes a realistic look at what it means to live in an abusive situation, and Jacqueline Wilson's *Lola Rose* deals with domestic violence and breast cancer. Kevin Brooks' *Martyn Pig* is about a boy who accidentally kills his alcoholic father; and the central character of Alan Gibbons' *Caught in the Crossfire* is Mike, who loves a British Muslim girl, while his younger brother gets involved with an organisation which wants a white Britain.

- Choose a theme, for example 'horses'.
- Sit down with a pen and a large piece of paper. Draw four concentric circles on the paper and divide them like a pie into eight sections.
- Outer ring: quickly write in each section a different kind of horse: cowboy's palomino? police horse? spotted pony in circus tinsel?
- Second ring: without referring to the horses, fill the sections with names of different landscapes, including the weather and season. A rainy autumn night in the back-end of Bristol? Snow-blizzard moors?
- Third ring: who is with the horses? Again, do not refer back, just describe the first character you think of in the first available space: a fat woman with long red nails and a mobile phone? a would-be jockey? a butcher?
- Inner ring: where is the child protagonist? At home in a boarding-house on the seafront? In a hospital bed? Buying a record in a Virgin superstore? Crawling through a rock tunnel?
- Select a pie slice. Taking the randomly juxtaposed elements and, keeping the child as a central figure, start dreaming up connections. Might the child buying the record be the son of a butcher who is planning to export the circus pony to France? Write for twenty minutes without stopping.
- Devise some alternative plots. One could be a fantasy, another a thriller, a third social realism. Each narrative hare you set running will start up others.
- Now look at your plots through the eyes of a child, remembering the limitations of that viewpoint – and its advantages. Search for new and exciting incidents and links: it is a puzzle only you can solve …

PLOT

Aristotle says that plot is the first essential. Though he is discussing tragedy, his dictum also applies to children's writing from fairytales to modern teen novels. Children are greedy readers who want everything now. They will not continue for long if the story fails to grip.

Though it need not always be a rollercoaster, your plot is a journey, a ride, and its gears need to be shifted smoothly. A sentence describes an action. A new sentence elaborates on that action, or moves to another which, in the simplest kind of story, will initiate a scene. Transitions are made in a word ('later' or 'then') or a phrase ('the next day' or 'when she woke up'). Hansel and Gretel may be lost in their forest, but the child reader needs signposts.

A different typeface can also be used as a signal, as in Peggy Parish's *Amelia Bedelia* (for six- to eight-year-olds), where the heroine is a cleaner who hilariously misinterprets her boss's instructions, which are in a font which looks like handwriting. Longer stories can use chapters to signal a new episode, to slacken or heighten tension, or show the passage of time. Fiction for older readers can even be written from different points of view. Aidan Chambers' *Postcards From No Man's Land* (for nine- to twelve-year-olds) commutes between a series of postcards written by a contemporary (boy) teenager visiting Amsterdam and the first-person story of a (girl) teenager living in Holland in 1944, with her name at the head of each chapter. Flashbacks likewise work for older readers, demonstrating shifts in time and the pressure of the past on the present; but they need to be vivid and clearly signalled.

For practice with plotting, read the section 'If you are stuck for a plot' in Chapter 6, 'Short story writing', then tackle the exercise that follows.

- Think of a simply structured story you enjoyed (for example, Little Red Riding Hood).
- Briefly describe the established ground (the home, the forest, Red Riding Hood's cottage).
- Decide on the catalyst (Red Riding Hood's mother sends her to visit her sick grandmother).
- Note down the nature of the quest (Red Riding Hood must cross the forest and deliver the scones).
- Think about whose action endangers the quest (the wolf throws a stone in the pool). Remember that obstacles often come in threes, in ascending order of danger.
- Decide what your heroine needs to do to reach her goal (the more passionate her efforts, and the greater the cost of failure, the more your reader or listener will be caught up in the story).

- What is the climax? (Do the wolf and the woodcutter fight it out – in a modern version – or are the grandmother and Red Riding Hood eaten?)
- Consider the mood of your ending or its moral (never stray from the path) to give your reader a 'come-down' time. Younger readers, when asked, claim to prefer happy endings; but older ones can accept a complex or bitter-sweet conclusion as more 'life-like'.

CHARACTER

While not wanting to deprive children of fairytales, many adults now feel that heroines such as Snow White and the Sleeping Beauty are too passive and conformist. Why not follow contemporary writers such as Tanith Lee who uses the excellent plots of fairytales while subverting their stereotypes? Though character comes second to plot, even younger readers like well-defined and plausible story people given the scope to feel and act. As Kit Spring put it in a recent book review, 'Children's fiction is full of central characters who overcome obstacles to complete the adventure, sort their lives out.'

Though aware that not every child enjoys being frightened, Marina Warner claims that 'uttering the fear, describing the phantom, generally scaring oneself and the audience constitutes one way of dealing with the feelings that giants, ogres, child-guzzlers, ghouls, vampires, cannibals, and all their kind inspire'. These malevolent creatures are at least as important as heroes, partly because they are stand-ins for the reader's dark side. As Patricia Duncker says, '[our parents] are the first people who own us, rule us, thwart us', and at times they make us feel murderous, a feeling which grows all the stronger if we are made to feel guilty for having it. When children are overwhelmed by a sense of their own 'badness', stories allow them to see that badness is only part of the story.

Your villain will need strong motives and a personality with which your protagonist can battle. Because children love the weak to outwit the strong – over and over again – success should never seem like a foregone conclusion: giants are famously hard to slay; Cinderella's sisters stay bullies to the end.

- Create a hero (or heroine). Their age should be at the top of your target range.
- Decide what they want and why (an imaginative or generous aim will grip your reader more quickly than a narrow one).
- Choose a dynamic antagonist and work out why they wish to thwart your hero.

- What qualities will your hero need to overcome the antagonist?
- Give your hero a helper. It could be an animal, a talisman or a human companion.
- Devise a dramatic high spot where the achievement of your protagonist's goal is in question. Make sure that their actions determine the outcome.

LANGUAGE

Never talk down to your readers: nothing is surer to make them abandon your book. Children have not yet had adult experiences, nor acquired the vocabulary to express them, but they can still be rude, suggestive, pompous, convoluted, blasphemous, funny ... depending on temperament. In the first pages of Philip Pullman's *Northern Lights* we encounter the words dais, daemon, Tokay, chafing-dish and Aerodock, none of them with explanatory notes, and all glittering with promise.

Avoid long speeches and the passive voice. In even the simplest tale, dialogue must develop plot and character. The ugly sisters declare themselves selfish and vain with their every command. The Fairy Godmother proves her inventiveness by sending Cinderella for household objects then changing them into something wonderful. Each character should have their own way of speaking: the wolf should not sound like the woodcutter. Do not be afraid to invent a type of speech which suits him.

- A girl is persuading another girl to ride her bike on waste ground which is off limits. Write their dialogue, including a dare or a bet – both common currency among children.
- Now write their conversation after the first girl has won the bet or dare; or the second has come to grief.
- Write a monologue for each girl as she leaves.
- Now write diary entries for both girls, or their thoughts while falling asleep.
- Change the characters' genders, then mix them. Bring in the parents. What version of events do the children tell them? What are their reactions?

RESEARCH

Publishing is a hard, market-driven business, and you need to keep abreast. Read as many children's books as possible, and use bookshops and the internet to find out what is selling well and which books have won prizes. Talk to librarians about current trends. Most libraries carry a copy of Lancashire County Council's booklet, *Children's Book of the Year Award,* in which books for twelves to fourteens are reviewed by fourteen-year-olds. Check their comments against your own. You could also offer to help out with the literacy hour or reading time at your local school, or become a volunteer at a youth club.

Children enjoy reading broadly as well as deeply, and need to know that their way of life is only one among many. Read stories and watch films about children in other cultures. You will not necessarily replicate their plots, but you will get a feel for how they work. Browse through newspapers from foreign countries. Even relatively unknown languages will yield something: you are putting yourself in the place of a child, perusing worlds not fully understood, learning from a picture, or a word you half-recognise. Pay attention to news stories about children and the way the media treats them. Does our society cherish children? What do *you* feel about them?

CONCLUSION

Above all else you need to keep listening to children: to the ways they speak to their teachers, to you, to each other; to their dialects, idiolects and slang, their buzz words and passions. Listen to the music they listen to. You may hear in its lyrics the language children admire and aspire to more often than the language they speak; but if you tap into its enormous energy you will find the emotional tone that your writing needs to capture.

Chances are that today's children are more savvy and sassy than you were, and familiar with things you did not know about until later. Try out your writing on them whenever you can. They are usually honest critics, and will say when your work fails to grip – and when, thanks to your hard-won skill, your story enthrals them.

15 REDRAFTING AND EDITING

Jenny Newman

'Anyone can write – and almost everyone you meet these days is writing. However, only the writers know how to rewrite. It is this ability alone that turns the amateur into a pro.'

William C. Knott

INTRODUCTION

As a writer you need time for inspiration, for getting in touch with your unconscious. Your first draft is a good place for going out on a limb, for fathoming new feelings, or trying out a fresh tone of voice without being monitored. This may mean shutting out your inner censor (Virginia Woolf called hers 'the Angel in the House') and letting yourself write as unselfconsciously, freely and fluently as you can.

But the creative process needs more than inspiration. As Tolstoy put it, 'In a writer there must always be two people – the writer and the critic.' At a certain point you must draw a line under what you have written, put it in your desk drawer, and groom the dog or make a pot of tea. The longer you can bring yourself to leave your first draft to one side without looking at it the better, but a week – or even a day or two – is far preferable to no time at all.

If you are a student, you may be writing to a tight schedule. Try, all the same, to leave yourself time to reread and amend your work before handing it in. If you write on a word-processor, print out your work before you revise. Reading a screen is hard on the eyes, so mistakes are easier to miss than they are on paper. Or, if you have grown word blind, record your work and listen through headphones while you go for a walk or do the chores. This is the first step towards becoming your own editor, or rather editors, because the all-important process of revision has several steps.

Throughout this chapter, 'to redraft' means to revise in the more comprehensive, thoroughgoing way typical of the early stages of the revision process, and 'to edit' means to pay close attention to detail and fine-tuning when the work is nearing completion.

REAL WRITING IS REWRITING

The process of redrafting that you may, in the beginning, find tedious, is precisely that extra effort which will make your work gripping to read, hear or see. It can be fun too, as a better version starts taking shape. Only an inexperienced writer dumps his work on someone else's desk for the final, crucial review, the one that often makes the difference between success and failure, acceptance and rejection.

To rewrite is to become a good parent to your work, seeing it through all the stages of its development. Checking facts, looking for spelling mistakes, clichés and repetition, or fiddling with commas and semi-colons is only part of it. During revision you learn new techniques, tackle problems of structure, and uncover the meaning of your work. This is why one rewrite is seldom enough, as is shown by the following interview, quoted by Bernays and Painter (1995):

Interviewer: How much rewriting do you do?
Hemingway: It depends. I rewrote the ending to *Farewell to Arms*, the last page of it, thirty-nine times before I was satisfied.
Interviewer: Was there some technical problem there? What was it that stumped you?
Hemingway: Getting the words right.

When you are struggling to 'get the words right' do not overlook your potential readers. You may already be in a workshop group with ground rules for considering draft material (if not, see Appendix A, 'The workshop'). Or you may already have trusted readers on whose opinion you depend. It is now that they come in useful, not when the work is burnished and comma perfect. Remember also that you are in charge and may have an overview that they cannot share.

REVISING FOR MEANING

This is the most involving, demanding and important form of revision, and may be partly a question of trusting your intuition. Contrary to popular belief, the meaning of what you write is not necessarily something you start with; nor does it always pop fully formed into your first draft. Flannery O'Connor is only one of many who talk about the process of writing as an act of discovery. Meaning may take shape over several drafts, or you may, halfway through, have a nagging sense that something has been left unsaid, without knowing quite what it is. Raymond Carver (1986) feels his revisions take him slowly into the heart of what the story is about. 'If the writing cannot be made as good as it is within us to make it, then why do it? In the end, the satisfaction of having done our best, and the proof of that labour, is the one thing we can take into the grave.' Revision, he believes, is about refusing to settle for less than the best you can do.

Finding your window

When you think you have finished, ask yourself the question, 'What is my poem, story or script about?' And then ask yourself, 'What is it really about?' If you cannot respond briefly and lucidly, it may be a sign that you need to spend more time clarifying your subject matter to yourself. Do as Stanley Elkin suggests, and 'after five or six drafts, write what [your] story means in one sentence. Then use that sentence to cut, revise, add, adjust, or change the next draft. Use that sentence as a filter, or a window, to the whole piece.'

REVISING FOR CHARACTER

The novelist Sue Gee says that character is all. Certainly readers and viewers like vigorous, well-drawn story people. Often this stage in revision means listening to your misgivings. You may sense, for instance, that your characters are not as compelling as they could be, but be unable to see why. This section is *not* a formula for when you write, or to be taken as proof that your story is lacking; it is simply a series of points for you to ponder.

If your heroine obstinately refuses to come to life, you have not clarified what she wants. Have you got a good antagonist to stop her getting it? Consider giving her a detailed past, even if it does not all appear in the script or story. Knowing a person's history alters your understanding of who she is today. Imagine your response to a loudmouth at a party – until you hear that she has just come from three years in solitary confinement.

Young writers in particular are prone to set their dramas in student flats. Why not give your character some kind of employment? You could base it on a job of your own, or research a likely career (books on work often make compelling reading), or else hang around somebody else's workplace, taking notes (see Chapter 1, 'The writer's notebook'). Your character's work can shape his perceptions, and give you a store of unusual metaphors for his vision of existence.

Many writers secretly feel that their characters are their slaves. Nevertheless, to the reader the characters must look as though they are driving the action. Do they wait like puppets to be jerked into life, or do they quarrel with each other, fall in love, gossip behind each other's backs, try and stop each other from getting what they want from a variety of motives, good and bad? When you are redrafting, scrutinise their functions: protagonist, antagonist, catalyst, love interest, helper, confidant, danger point, or means of providing contrast. Have they all got something to do? If they double up, can they be cut? Or, alternatively, is there a character missing?

Few stories or scripts have space to develop every character, so many writers depend on stereotypes (the unflappable nurse, the bossy teacher) for the walk-on roles that the viewer or reader needs to recognise quickly. But if your main character is a dumb body-builder or a wily East End barrow boy, your reader may feel that she knows him already, and lose her wish to read on. You may, of course, enjoy overturning such stereotypes, as Anita Brookner does through her novelist heroine in *Hotel du Lac*.

Whether the character is major or minor, check that the dialogue is taut and well constructed, and that it serves a purpose besides conveying information. Try and give all your characters distinct voices and speech patterns, and do not call the two main ones Harry and Henry. Distinctive names beginning with different letters will help your reader keep track of who is who.

REVISING FOR PACE

There is no one way to pace a piece of writing. Chekhov suggested that you write a beginning, middle and end, then cut the beginning and the end. Dangerous advice, perhaps – but if you have read Chekhov's stories you may see some of its advantages. Many script writers have likewise proposed that you enter your scene as late as possible and leave it as early as you can, like the short story writer Raymond Carver ('Get in, get out. Don't linger. Go on'). When you revisit that crucial beginning, ask yourself if your story starts too slowly. In the first draft, openings are often just 'throat-clearing' and can be scrapped at a later stage; or else they can be redrafted or even written at the very end.

If you sense that the structure sags in the middle, ask if the line through your story is clear. If in doubt, try writing it out in one paragraph, and see if anything is missing. Is the conflict and tension sustained? Do you have the right balance between dialogue and action? Scripts, novels and short stories can all be ruined by too many 'talking heads'. List your main plot points and check they are in the right order (that is, going from smaller to larger, with cause followed by effect). Do they hinge on a need or desire in the mind of your central character? Is there enough at stake? You can always tighten a story by 'putting a clock in it'. Think of *High Noon* or *The Silence of the Lambs* or any other film or book which kept you on the edge of your seat with its race against time. Such plots are not weighed down by too much flashback, especially early on; nor are there too many subplots to detract from the main action. Yet every reader or viewer needs the occasional breather. Fiction writers know many methods – such as description, or the use of retrospect – of slowing the pace. Even the tensest film script should be spiked with scenes that vary the rhythm, by focusing, for example, on atmosphere or character development.

Every piece of writing has its own momentum, and after the struggle to get started, and plot the middle, you may find that the last third is downhill all the way. This is why it is tempting to rush. But the stronger the story, the more your reader or viewer will feel cheated if you skimp on the turning point or resolution. Ask yourself if anything has changed. Most importantly, has your protagonist learnt something, whether pleasing or painful?

Placing the final full stop is always a delicate matter. If the ending feels hurried, ask yourself if the climax comes out of nowhere, or is it brought about by your main character? Does it have an internal logic, following on from your previous plot points?

On the other hand, if your finale seems flat, see if you have written past your ending, and given your reader not one but two conclusions.

REVISING FOR STYLE

The poet and the scriptwriter are opposites. The poet redrafts in solitude, and can make the amendments which please him, down to the last semicolon. If a poem is altered without his permission by, say, a magazine editor, he will have the right to complain. A poet may not be paid much, but over his work he reigns supreme.

A writer for a television soap is part of a team. For her, revision can mean letting a script go: to script editors who prune and alter it, to producers, directors and eventually to actors. Writing for television is not a solitary but a collaborative act.

Yet these diverse writers share one key belief: that each word counts. This is why both must revise ruthlessly. For the poet, the medium's intensity means that he must weigh every word, test every image, scrutinise his use of metre and his line endings; and the short story writer too may take as much care as the poet. The screenwriter, on the other hand, may not share such scrupulous attention to detail; yet she is up against limits of time, space and the production business, where every word costs money, and must therefore have maximum impact. Both kinds of writer must learn how to 'murder their darlings'.

Few writers in any medium find that good style happens by accident: it develops little by little from your first rough notes to your final version. Jeanette Winterson uses the analogy of the acrobat: years of practice go into one single, seemingly effortless movement. Your goal is not to make writing effortless, but to make it look effortless. Underline your first interesting line or sentence. If it is not the first one, or very near it, why not?

Surplus words and phrases are not just an extra your reader can choose to discard. They distract from your whole style, and leech the life even from those words that are well chosen.

In particular, watch out for the following creative minefields:

- Overkill, such as lists of adjectives; or laying on so many details that you lessen credibility. Chekhov believed it was an insult to over-describe; the writer should give just enough detail to evoke the reader's knowledge of life. Elmore Leonard says, 'I try to leave out the parts that people skip', which is another way of saying that in writing less often means more. Sometimes you need the guts to cut.
- Showing off at your reader's expense. Aim to be straightforward and exact rather than too high-flown.
- Predictable noun-adjective combinations such as 'bitter pill' or 'clear blue sky'.
- Overuse of adverbs. A strong, expressive verb, such as 'drift', 'mooch' or 'slouch' may be more telling than 'walk slowly'. Or, rather than *telling* us that your hero reads incessantly, *show* us his red-rimmed eyes.
- Redundant words, as in the following phrases: 'appreciate in value', 'rack and ruin', 'hope for the future', 'I personally'. Compile your own list of surplus expressions.
- Fussy, overcomplicated punctuation.
- Meaningless terms such as 'in point of fact', 'at the end of the day' and 'lo and behold'.
- Weak intensifiers such as very, really, extremely and exceptionally.
- Overworked similes ('green as grass') and metaphors ('dyed in the wool').
- Misattributions, such as 'she clutched the receiver in one hand, while with the other she nibbled a sandwich' (with the tiny teeth in her palm?).

REVISING FOR ACCURACY

Theatres, magazines, production companies and publishing houses are bombarded with submissions from hopeful writers. Who, in these cost-conscious days, would spend valuable time struggling with a badly laid-out script, or choose an ill-punctuated, misspelt novel over one which is comma-perfect? Attention to detail suggests a professionalism and pride in your work which goes well beyond mere pedantry.

In an Isaac Babel short story the narrator says, 'no iron can pierce the heart with such force as a full stop put in just the right place'. Punctuation is an aspect of meaning, telling your reader how your sentences are paced, and clarifying the rhythm of your prose. In poetry it creates vital tension, overriding or corroborating your line length and stanza form. If you are unsure of the rules, find a recent edition of G. V. Carey's *Mind the Stop* (Carey, 1976) and keep it on your desk.

Always check your facts. If you misspell a street name in Harare, or your character's flight out of Gander is delayed by snow at the wrong time of year, you may lost the confidence of your readers or audience. Consult Appendix B, 'Writing from research', for sources of information, and build a collection of reference books on the areas you write about, plus *The Oxford Style Manual,* a good thesaurus, and a dictionary. The complete *Oxford English Dictionary* will soon be available on the web at most good libraries, where it will be regularly updated, or you may, if you wish, become a subscriber yourself.

CONCLUSION

Be methodical about keeping your drafts. If you use a word-processor, copy your work each time you start to rewrite, and print out regularly; otherwise you will be left with only one version, and no record of how you reached it. It is possible to revise too much, and knowing when to stop takes practice. Sometimes first thoughts are best thoughts, and later drafts can lose conviction and freshness. But more new writers stop too soon than go on too long.

16 GETTING PUBLISHED, PRODUCED OR PERFORMED

Jenny Newman,

Edmund Cusick and

Aileen La Tourette

INTRODUCTION

There is no guarantee that your writing, however brilliant, will be what publishers or producers are looking for at any given time. Success depends on a number of factors: talent, perseverance and a knowledge of your potential market – not forgetting good luck. But there are better and worse ways of trying to place a piece of work and, at the very least, you can avoid some mistakes which will only succeed in wasting your time and that of other people.

HOW TO SUBMIT YOUR WORK

First of all, research your market. If you are a poet or short story writer, for example, read as many relevant magazines as you can. They may be expensive, but your local bookshop will probably stock some of them, and your library may order them if you ask. Scour *The Writer's and Artist's Yearbook* and *The Writer's Handbook* for outlets, see how the magazines describe themselves, and decide if your work is suitable. Keep an eye open for magazines just starting up. They will be on the lookout for new writers to fill their pages. If you are a poet, try to visit the Poetry

Library on London's South Bank, which stocks a wide range of publications. Some poetry-reading venues have 'open mike' sessions where people read from the floor, and where you may make useful contacts and be given informal feedback. Look at poetry listings in *Time Out*, or check your local press to see where the readings are being held. Showing your face at local gatherings is a good way to get to know the poetry scene.

You can also consult the world wide web, where most magazines have up-to-date and informative sites. You can email poems, short stories and even novels around the world, so the process of submitting is much less cumbersome. Increasingly, ezines are a possible market, and the American market, for instance, has many more openings for short stories than the UK. Some prestigious web-based magazines are read by publishers and agents worldwide. Consult Chapter 13, 'Writing on the web', on how to research outlets. You might also want to consider designing your own website and updating it regularly as a way of promoting and showcasing your work. Have a look at some well-known writers' sites for ideas and information.

Do not neglect competitions. They help you impose a deadline on yourself, and can get your creative juices flowing. Many short story and poetry competitions run each year, some linked to bookshops, colleges or literary festivals, others in magazines: either glossy, like *Cosmopolitan*, or smaller and more local. Competitions are especially important to poets. Enter your work as widely as possible, reading the judges' work beforehand to get a sense of their preferences. *The Writer's News* and *The New Writer* usually publicise competitions, and the Arts Council publishes comprehensive listings. Your regional arts board will have a mailing list, and it is worth ringing up and putting your name on it. They may run courses and competitions of their own, and will know what is happening in your area. Anything which gets your work seen and read by other people is good. If you win or are placed even in a small competition, you will – at the very least – have something to put in your covering letter the next time you send your work out.

If you have written a novel, your best chance of finding a publisher is through a literary agent, though competition to be taken on is almost as fierce as it is to be published. Sometimes an agent will leave a big agency to start up on their own. They will be looking for new clients, so comb through *The Writer's and Artist's Yearbook* and *The Writer's Handbook*, and look out for relevant items in *The Writer's News*. If you send your work directly to a publisher or publishers, again consult *The Writer's and Artist's Yearbook* and also *The Small Press Guide* for specialist, community and local publishers, and for new presses starting out. Keep up to date with your favourite authors, browse in your local bookshop, look at titles and blurbs, read first chapters, comb the review pages, and see who publishes books similar to yours.

Before committing your work to the post, make a phone call or send an email to find out a name – not a company, or a network, but the name of an individual – to whom you can send it. Make sure you know precisely what they want: possibly just a brief synopsis and two or three chapters in the first instance, rather than a whole book.

Can you send the same manuscript to several agents or publishers at once? The short answer is yes. The market is tough and you too have to be tough. But be warned that there are some agents who will not read any material not submitted to them exclusively.

When submitting screenplays or scripts for television or radio plays, you will find that different producers want different things. Sometimes it is only a single page of ideas. Sometimes it is a more traditional four- or five-page treatment. Sometimes, though rarely, it is a whole script. Make sure you know what the producer is looking for. Get a name by ringing the company to which you are submitting. There may be someone who will chat to you about their requirements. Do not assume you have to begin with a full-length feature film. There are competitions run by Channel 4, the BBC, the British Film Institute and the British Academy of Film and Television Arts (BAFTA) for short films. Ring them and ask them to send you information. Again, try your regional arts boards and the Arts Council. Also bear in mind that local drama groups sometimes want someone to film their work. Hospitals or local councils may need documentary films. Any work you do will help you learn your craft. Check your local paper for coming events and ring up to see if the organisers might like a video of the day or evening.

Plays can be performed in church halls or above pubs as well as in theatres. Contact local drama groups and ask if they are looking for material. Go to the theatre as much as you can, and find out what kind of work a given artistic director tends to support before you send them anything. Many large theatres have studios which put on plays by lesser-known playwrights. The Writer's Guild currently has a special student rate and knows which companies are soliciting scripts, and also about local, national and international play competitions. Rehearsed readings are a good way to get an audience for a new play, and are far cheaper than a full performance.

When you are ready to submit your work, use paper clips, not staples, and print on one side only of A4 paper, following the relevant format (double-spaced for short stories and novels). Number your pages, and add your title or some of it to every page. Do not wrap each page in a plastic folder – they fall across editors' desks in slippery heaps. Include a stamped, self-addressed envelope and make sure the postage is correct. In the case of a screenplay, check whether it might be better to send a treatment. Add a covering letter saying a little about yourself and detailing, briefly, any other work you have had published, produced or performed. Be methodical. Note down what you have sent and where – and then try to forget about it. The best of all possible therapies during the inevitable waiting period is to embark on a new piece of work.

FEEDBACK

As it says in Appendix A, 'The workshop', rejection is the base from which most writers start, so try not to feel too discouraged when your precious work lands back on the mat with a thud. Devise strategies for coping with disappointment, and try – especially if you are a poet or a short story writer – to keep several pieces in circulation at once. Compile a list of targeted publications and tick them off as you go, making it your policy to turn your work around fast.

Pay attention to what people say. There is not much you can learn from a rejection slip, but sometimes an editor will scribble a few words on it. Read them. There are degrees and stages of rejection and acceptance. Agents, publishers and artistic directors are busy people, and any words of encouragement they give you should be taken seriously. If they say keep in touch, keep in touch. Send them the next thing you write.

Keep trying, and learn to be resourceful. There are many ways of promoting your work, and you may even invent some yourself. Do not isolate yourself. Writers need other writers, as Appendix A points out. Create support networks for yourself. We can learn from each other's successes and failures as well as from our own, and can share our highs and lows as we go. You may have a good spell, or a bad one, at any point in your writing career. There is no corporate ladder to climb rung by rung. There is no structure as such.

CONCLUSION

Celebrate your victories, however small. They mean something. Be generous with yourself. You are your own employer as well as your own employee. Take breaks when you need them. Do not work until you are drained or exhausted. Do not berate yourself if a piece of work comes back. Be sympathetic, as you would be with someone else. It sounds obvious, but sometimes we have a tendency to flagellate ourselves when we fall short of our own expectations. Keep your expectations realistic and develop your own strategies for dealing with the ups and downs of a writer's life.

Conclusion

You will not become a famous writer – or a writer at all – instantly. It will take time, and there will be frustrations along the way. Most writers learn to live with a certain amount of rejection. The important thing is to keep writing, and to keep pushing your work out when it and you are ready.

You have read the advice in this book, and tried out the techniques. But never be afraid to develop your own methods, and always work at your own pace. Do not rush your writing. It deserves the best chance you can give it.

Above all, do not be discouraged. You are engaged in a creative activity which is absorbing and inspiring. The creative process itself is valuable and worthwhile, and the time you spend on it will never be wasted. If you have any talent, and persevere, you will break through eventually. Be patient, be willing to work hard, and enjoy the marvellous path you have chosen for yourself. Bon voyage!

APPENDIX A: THE WORKSHOP

Edmund Cusick

WHY JOIN A WORKSHOP?

Writing can be a lonely business. Rejection is base camp, the point from which most writers – including your own heroes and heroines – set out towards the summit. Being part of a group where others are starting to climb can be a huge help.

To dream of writing the perfect piece straight off is like prospecting in the hope of finding not just a nugget, but a piece of gold miraculously formed into a ring. As Chapter 15, 'Redrafting and editing', said, writing is as much about reworking as it is about the first rush of inspiration. No matter how tough and self-critical you try to be, many of your strengths and weaknesses will remain invisible to you. To improve your work you need critics: not carping, antagonistic faultfinders, but people who know about literature because they care about it. The most helpful will be those who have themselves embarked on the lifelong apprenticeship that is writing.

Criticism is not a magic wand guaranteed to make your work perfect. Your critics may simply be wrong. If, however, you get a similar response from different readers, then chances are they have noticed something you have missed. If you in turn apply yourself to other people's work, struggling to identify not only what may need correction but how you would correct it, you will be honing your own critical skill, your gift for literary problem solving: sharpening your nose for the right word, the right rhythm, the best sentence structure. When you return to your own work, you will be a better writer for it.

FINDING A WORKSHOP

Students on creative writing courses generally have access to workshops. If you are on your own, the search for a writers' group may take a while. The important thing is not just to find a workshop, but to find one that is right for you. This may not be the nearest, or the one that says the 'nicest' things about your writing, or that promises to boost your social life. It will be the one where you find people of similar dedication and seriousness to yourself: people who share your need to read as well as write.

Groups exist for different reasons. Some are collections of friends, some are organised and run by professional writers or paid tutors. Some promote a particular type of writing. Some use writing as therapy. Some are exclusive, asking prospective members to submit work to show they meet a required standard, while others are happy to welcome anyone. Some are mercilessly analytical, while in others everyone gets a round of applause for the courage they have shown in just being prepared to come along and read.

Look for information on local writing groups in libraries, writing magazines, bookshops, your regional arts board, university lifelong-learning departments and notice boards in colleges. Try all the suitable-sounding groups you come across. The first you visit is unlikely to be the best one for you. The test is not, did it make me feel wonderful? but, did it help me to write better?

PREPARATION FOR FEEDBACK

Before you look at other people's work, read some published writing. This gets your eye in for what works and what does not, and reminds you of the standards you wish to reach.

You could suggest a poem or story to your group, and let everyone comment on one feature they feel is well done, and one which could be improved. If you establish the qualities you value before you look at each other's writing, you will find it easier to be objective and precise.

Once you have looked at a range of published work, try collectively to devise a list of features which most people agree are good qualities or faults in writing. You may not reach a consensus, but the discussion will itself clarify the task facing the workshop.

HANDLING FEEDBACK

Agree in advance what your method will be, so that everyone feels they are being treated fairly. Workshops are opportunities to learn, not arenas for praise or condemnation. Aim to describe the work's individual features, rather than pronouncing a verdict – like Roman emperors at the games, or ice-skating judges. Make sure that everyone who speaks finds one thing that is done well and one thing that could be done better. There is no place for destructive criticism. Comments which dismiss the work without offering a creative solution derive from a lazy attitude and a lack of commitment to what a workshop can achieve.

All work submitted is in a sense work in progress and part of your development as a writer. The workshop is better for sampling your readers' impressions than for debating them, and the importance of listening, rather than leaping in to defend yourself, cannot be overestimated. It is all too easy to be distracted by a single comment – helpful or unhelpful – and to miss other observations, so you might want to record the workshop, or ask someone in the group to keep a note of the gist of what is said. Remember this is only the point of harvest. The exercise becomes useful when you take the comments home and run them through the mill of your own thoughts.

CONCLUSION

Never confuse the means – regular contact with a group of writers – with the end: improving your writing. In the course of your writing life you may associate with several groups. You, or other members, may outgrow a particular workshop and seek a more demanding forum. This will be part of your creative development. Approach any workshop in a spirit of sincere and open criticism and support, and the time you spend there will benefit all who attend it.

APPENDIX B: WRITING FROM RESEARCH

Dymphna Callery

A work of literature is a world unto itself, but to ring true it needs to reflect carefully chosen aspects of the so-called real world. As Ernest Hemingway says, 'A writer who omits things because he does not know them only makes hollow places in his writing.' Finding out about what you do not know broadens your horizons and liberates your fiction, script or poem from the dangers of being too self-involved or self-enclosed. Your passion for a subject will not only drive your investigations but colour your writing, making it more gripping for the reader.

FORMS OF RESEARCH

Getting started

Hemingway maintained that seeing and listening were the two funda-mental attributes necessary to the writer. Your eyes and ears are your basic research tools, plus the habit of attention, and the use of your writer's notebook as described in Chapter 1. Learn to process the infor-mation that comes through your senses, and to practise awareness wher-ever you are. Developing a nose for interesting material will keep your writer's notebook full and mean you will never be stuck for 'something to write about'. Note down whatever interests you, and also why, and what you feel about it. Your raw material is essentially the study of human beings and their relationship to each other, to the world, and to what goes on around them.

Geographical research

Go to the place you are writing about and/or check maps, the web and the records of people who have visited it. Read Chapter 12 on 'Travel writing', and do not neglect fictional accounts, if there are any. Even if you cannot afford to fly to Shanghai, you might manage a visit to the nearest China Town or a local Chinese restaurant. Wherever you go and whatever you taste, see, hear or read, you are looking for the particular, sometimes quirky, items that will fuel your imagination. The right ones may take time to uncover, but they will be worth it.

Historical research

Writers have always borrowed from the past, and distance can help rather than hinder our vision of a person or an event. Shakespeare, for example, lifted, then transformed, dozens of stories which existed in an earlier form. Like an actor, you will sometimes need to improvise, putting yourself in the shoes of people in far-flung places and situations. For this you need a reservoir of knowledge about both individuals and period. You will not draw on it all directly but, like the invisible nine-tenths of an iceberg, it will enrich your work.

The Public Records Office in Kew is a favourite haunt of writers, with its records of parish registers, schools, and births and deaths, going back several centuries. You can write to the PRO, but a visit may stimulate you in unexpected ways. The USA National Archives and Records Administration site can be accessed on http//www.naragov. Museums and art galleries help with period detail. Graveyards offer the writer a great deal, not least a fund of names. Read Chapter 14 for advice on researching on the web, a vast source of information. Never ignore serendipity.

Biographical research

If you are fascinated by a particular figure you need to find out everything about them. The *Dictionary of National Biography* is a comprehensive work of reference, and Ann Hoffmann's *Research for Writers* contains a helpful chapter on other sources for biographical research. Sheila Yeger (1990) describes how handling something your character has touched can inspire you in quite a different way from reading about them. Visiting their home(land), consulting their letters and writings, will also help, but do not get overwhelmed. You are *interpreting* a life, and using information imaginatively to create something new.

The horse's mouth

People are a great resource. If your play is set on a boat, research on the spot may prove more useful than reading a book. If you want to write about drug smuggling, talk to Customs and Excise officials; or you may need to meet dock workers or people involved in the criminal justice system. This may mean trips to open court sessions, and more formal interviews with solicitors and barristers. Court records appear in newspapers and may be consulted in archives, but firsthand accounts from those caught up in the process may be more vivid.

Develop a good interviewing technique. Preparation is essential, and your interview will be more productive if you bring a list of questions, though you also need to be open to what people want to say. Save your key questions until well into the interview. Taping conversations is the best method, as you will often forget key points, or find yourself scribbling instead of listening. However, some people are nervous of being recorded and the machine may inhibit them. Try getting them relaxed in a friendly manner first, and then ask if you can record the conversation.

An ethical note

Be sensitive if you are drawing on contemporary sources, and take time to consider your motives. Hemingway said that he had 'a wonderful novel to write about Oak Park and would never do it because I did not want to hurt living people' (Phillips, 1984). If you can, ask permission to use someone's story, treat it sensitively, and be honest about why it appeals to you. Your sources will be justified in feeling angry and abused if you misrepresent them or make fun of their emotions and vulnerability.

The ethics of taking factual events and weaving fictional stories around them depend to a certain extent on a lapse of time: the closer we are to an event, the more we seem to demand total accuracy; the further away, the more poetic licence we allow. Yet sometimes it is the writer's vision which allows the reader or spectator to gain insight into a deeper truth as opposed to mere verisimilitude.

Above all, allow yourself time to digest information; otherwise your writing will be dominated by the process rather than fuelled by it. Research is there to be enjoyed as part of the adventure of becoming a writer.

Select bibliography

Armitage, Simon and Maxwell, Glyn. *Moon Country*. London: Faber & Faber, 1996.

Ash, William. *The Way to Write Radio Drama*. London: Elm Tree Books, 1985.

Ashe, Geoffrey. *Mythologies of the British Isles*. London: Guild, 1991.

Beckett, Samuel. *The Complete Dramatic Works*. London: Faber & Faber, 1990.

Bell, Julia and Magrs, Paul (eds.). *The Creative Writing Coursebook*. London: Macmillan, 2001.

Bellonci, Maria. *The Travels of Marco Polo*, trans Teresa Waugh. New York: Facts on File Publications, 1984.

Bennett, Alan, *et al*. *Talking Heads (1 & 2)*. London: BBC Audiobooks, 1998.

Bernays, Anne and Painter, Pamela. *What If? Writing Exercises for Fiction Writers*. Revised and expanded edn. London: HarperCollins College Publishers, 1995.

Bickham, Jack M. *Writing the Short Story: A Hands-On Programme*. Cincinnati: Writer's Digest Books, 1994.

Bord, Janet and Colin. *Atlas of Magical Britain*. London: Sidgwick and Jackson, 1990.

Brande, Dorothea. *Becoming a Writer*. London: Macmillan, 1934; 1986 edn.

Brook, Peter. *The Empty Space*. London: Methuen, 1968.

Bryson, Bill. *Notes from a Small Island*. London: Black Swan, 1996.

Burroway, Janet. *Writing Fiction: A Guide to Narrative Craft*. New York: HarperCollins, 4th edn, 1996.

Butt, Maggie. 'Maximising Creativity'. *Writing in Education*, no. 22, spring 2001.

Carey, G. V. *Mind the Stop*. Cambridge: Cambridge University Press, 1939; reprinted Harmondsworth: Penguin, 1976.

Carter, Angela (ed.). *The Virago Book of Fairy Tales*. London: Virago, 1990.

Carter, Angela. *The Curious Room*. London: Vintage, 1997.

Carver, Raymond. 'On Writing', in *Fires*. London: Picador, 1986.

Carver, Raymond. *The Path to the Waterfall*. New York: HarvillCollins, 1989.

Chadwick, David. *Thank You and OK! An American Zen Failure in Japan*. London: Penguin/Arkana, 1994.

Champion, Sarah (ed). *Fortune Hotel: Twisted Travel Stories*. Harmondsworth: Penguin, 1999.

Chatwin, Bruce. *Songlines*. London: Picador, 1988.

Coles, Gladys Mary (ed). *The Poet's View: Poems for Paintings in the Walker Art Gallery*. West Kirby: Headland Publications, 1996.

Cousineau, Phil. *The Art of Pilgrimage*. Shaftesbury, Dorset: Element Books, 1999.

Culshaw, Chris and Thornes, Nelson. *Radio Riff-Raff*. London: New Spirals Plays, 2002.

De Botton, Alain. *The Art of Travel*. Harmondsworth: Penguin, 2003.

Duncker, Patricia. *Writing on the Wall: Selected Essays*. London: Pandora Press, 2002.

Esslin, Martin. *The Theatre of the Absurd*. Harmondsworth: Penguin, 1991.

Evans, David. 'A Poetry Reading on Riverside', in *Brought to Book: The Winners of the 1994 Ian St James Awards*. London: HarperCollins, 1994.

Evans, David. 'Sabbatical'. *Critical Quarterly*, vol. 30, no. 2, spring 1988.

Field, Syd. *Screenplay*. New York: Dell Publishing, 1982.

Friel, James. 'A Posthumous Affair', in *Pretext*, 2, 2000.

Gardner, John. *The Art of Fiction*. New York: Alfred A. Knopf, 1984.

Gellhorn, Martha. *Travels with Myself and Another*. London: Eland, 1978.

Goldman, William. *Adventures in the Screen Trade*. New York: Abacus, 1984.

Greene, Graham. *Twenty-One Stories*. Harmondsworth: Penguin, 1970.

Guralnick, Elissa S. *Sight Unseen: Beckett, Pinter, Stoppard and Other Contemporary Dramatists on Radio*. Athens, Ohio: Ohio University Press, 1996.

Hamilton-Paterson, James. *Playing with Water*. London: Granta Publications, 1998.

Hemingway, Ernest. *Death in the Afternoon*. 1938; Harmondsworth: Penguin, 1966.

Hemley, Robin. *Turning Life into Fiction*. Cincinnati: Story Press, 1994.

Hoffmann, Ann. *Research for Writers*. London: A. & C. Black, 4th edn, 1992.

Holgate, Andrew and Wilson-Fletcher, Honor (eds.). *The Test of Time: What Makes a Classic a Classic*. London: Waterstones Magazine Publication, 1999.

Horstmann, Rosemary. *Writing for Radio*. London: A&C Books, 1988.

Jung, Carl Gustav. *Man and his Symbols*. London: Picador, 1999.

Keatley, Charlotte. *My Mother Said I Never Should*. London: Methuen, 1994.

Lurie, Alison. *Don't Tell the Grown-Ups*. New York: Avon Books, 1990.

McKee, Robert. *Story*. London: Methuen, 1999.

Mamet, David. *A Whore's Profession*. London: Faber & Faber, 1994.

Matthiesen, F. O. and Murdoch, Kenneth B. (eds.). *The Notebooks of Henry James*. Chicago: University of Chicago Press, 2000.

Matthiessen, Peter. *The Snow Leopard*. London: Pan, 1975.

Mills, Paul. *Writing in Action*. London: Routledge, 1996.

Minshull, Duncan (ed.). *Telling Stories*, vol. 3. London: Sceptre, 1994.

Motion, Andrew and Morrison, Blake (eds.). *The Penguin Book of Contemporary British Poetry*. Harmondsworth: Penguin, 1982.

Nabokov, Vladimir. *Lectures on Literature*. New York and London: Harcourt Brace Jovanovich, 1980.

Newby, Eric. *A Book of Travellers' Tales*. London: Picador, 1989.

Novakovich, Josip. *The Fiction Writer's Workbook*. Cincinnati: Writer's Digest Books, 1998.

Oates, Joyce Carol (ed.). *The Oxford Book of American Short Stories*. Oxford: Oxford University Press, 1994.

O'Connor, Frank. *The Lonely Voice: A Study of the Short Story*. London: Macmillan, 1963.

O'Connor, Joseph. *Sweet Liberty: Travels in Irish America*. London: Picador, 1997.

O'Rourke, P. J. *Holidays in Hell*. London: Picador, 1989.

Ozick, Cynthia. *Writers at Work: The Paris Review Interviews, Eighth Series*. New York: VikingPenguin, 1988.

Phillips, Larry (ed.). *Hemingway on Writing*. London: Granada, 1984.

Pitt-Kethley, Fiona. 'Introduction', in *Classic Travel Stories*. London: Leopard, 1996.

Plimpton, George (ed.). *The Writer's Chapbook: Edited from the Paris Review Interviews*. New York: The Modern Library, 1999.

Polo, Marco. *The Travels of Marco Polo*. London: Sidgwick and Jackson, 1984.

Pritchett, V. S. (ed.). *The Oxford Book of Short Stories*. Oxford: Oxford University Press, 2001.

Queneau, Raymond. *Exercises in Style*. London: Marion Boyars, 1972.

Rayner, Tristine. *The New Diary: How to Use a Journal for Self Guidance and Expanded Creativity*. London: Angus and Robertson, 1986.

Rich, Deike and Begg, Ean. *On the Trail of Merlin: A Guide to the Celtic Mystery Tradition*. London: Aquarian Press, 1991.

Ritter, Robert M. (ed.). *The Oxford Style Manual*. Oxford: Oxford University Press, 2003.

St Aubin de Teran, Lisa (ed.). *The Virago Book of Wanderlust and Dreams*. London: Virago Press, 1988.

Sarton, May. *Journal of a Solitude*. London: Women's Press, 1985.

Sellers, Susan. *Taking Reality by Surprise: Writing for Pleasure and Publication*. London: Women's Press, 1991.

Shaughnessy, Susan (ed.). *Meditations for Writers*. London: HarperCollins, 1993.

Simpson, Joe. *Touching the Void*. London: Vintage, 1988.

Sumrall, Amber Coverdale (ed.). *Write to the Heart*. Freedom, Calif.: The Crossing Press, 1992.

Theroux, Paul. *The Happy Isles of Oceania*. New York: Balantine Books, 1992.

Thomas, R. S. *Autobiographies*. New York: VikingPhoenix, 1998.

Thomas, R. S. *Selected Prose*. Bridgend: Seren Books, 1992.

Turco, Lewis. *The New Book of Forms: A Handbook of Poetics*. Hanover and London: University Press of New England, 1986.

Uelan, Brenda. *If You Want to Write: Releasing Your Creative Spirit*. Shaftesbury, Dorset: Element Books, 1991.

Warner, Marina. *No Go the Bogeyman: Scaring, Lulling and Making Mock*. London: Chatto & Windus, 1998.

Woolf, Leonard (ed.). *A Writer's Diary: Being Extracts from the Diary of Virginia Woolf*. New York: Harcourt Brace, 1953.

Woolf, Virginia. 'Mr. Bennett and Mrs. Brown', in *The Captain's Deathbed and Other Essays*. London: The Hogarth Press, 1950.

Yeger, Sheila. *The Sound of One Hand Clapping: A Guide to Writing for the Theatre*. Oxford: Amber Lane Press, 1990.

INDEX